ESSAYS FROM A REALISTIC OPTIMIST

no time for small talk

AILEEN ROBBINS

Little Star

ESSAYS FROM A REALISTIC OPTIMIST

no time for small talk

Aileen Robbins

Little Star

Published by Little Star

For permission, write to the publisher Little Star
Richmond, Virginia
littlestar.com

Unless otherwise noted photos are the courtesy of Aileen Robbins
Edited by Constance Costas
Printed interior book and cover design by Wendy Daniel

ISBN: 978-1-7323915-5-0

Printed in the United States of America. First Edition.

For Ariel and Sage
"to my two best personal cheerleaders"

Contents

A Series of Nudges

A Series of Nudges

WHEN I WAS IN my forties and recently divorced, I took a long-overdue vacation to Aspen. On the flight, I was seated next to an impossibly handsome man. I greeted him warmly but was met with stony silence, which he maintained for the next three hours. Later, when I told my friend, Murry Sidlin, about my fruitless encounter with my potential next-husband, he came up with the perfect retort. "When you landed," he said, "you should have turned to him and said, 'Well! Enough about *me*…!'"

A great line, but the irony masked a lot of truth. Years ago, I would have felt uncomfortable talking or writing about myself. In the recent past, however, I've gotten over it. Everyone from my friends, to my therapist at Sloan Kettering, to complete strangers who've read my personal essay, *The Prednisone Princess Diaries*, has urged me to share my writing. And after several nudges over the past few decades, a sequence of events in the Spring of 2018 finally led me to put together this slim volume.

It all started with letters to Peter.

For the twenty-four years I co-ran my own marketing

company, I wrote for my clients: brochures, speeches, background stories, ad copy, press releases, and articles for wine and food publications and newspapers. I wrote about everything but myself — except in letters to my friend, Peter.

Peter Kazaras and I met in our twenties, at the start of our operatic careers. Even though our professional lives diverged, for around thirty-five years we have remained in constant touch. With his husband, Armin, and my daughter, Ariel; we've gone on vacations, shared life events, and spent holidays together.

To keep Peter up-to-date about what was going on in my life while he was traveling the country singing leading tenor role in major opera houses, I wrote him letters. This was in the days before email, when dinosaurs still roamed the earth. I would type three- to four-page personal letters and mail them wherever he was performing at the time. One day, he called me from Santa Fe to ask why I hadn't written?

"I sent you a long letter last week," I replied.

"Yes, but that was a week ago, and the cast keeps asking if I've received another letter from Aileen."

"What do you mean, *the cast?* How do they know about my letters?"

"Well, I used to read your letters to myself during lunch in the cafeteria. People would hear me laughing and, when they asked, I told them I was reading a letter from Aileen and then I'd read a few of the funny bits aloud. After a while, they insisted I read the whole letter. Now, they ask every few days whether I've received another one. When I didn't get one today, they sounded really disappointed."

"How could you do that?" I wailed, "my letters aren't meant to entertain a crowd; they're intimate reports on my life and how I'm trying to cope."

"That's what makes them so good," replied Peter. "You're not trying to be funny. But don't worry, nobody knows your last name."

"Small comfort!" I shrieked. "They're bound to figure it out; I'm flying to Santa Fe in two weeks. How were you planning to introduce me — with an alias?"

"Oh, that's right!" exclaimed Peter. "They'll be so excited to finally meet you!" Part of me was horrified that my life was being broadcast to the Santa Fe opera community, but another part was surprised and pleased that I'd found an appreciative audience.

There was another person to whom I told everything: Brook and I have been friends since kindergarten at the Brearley School in New York City. At nineteen, Brook married and moved to Washington. Later, she divorced and moved to California. We stayed in touch through marathon weekly phone conversations, often spending Saturday nights chatting from opposite coasts, for the approximate duration of a relaxed dinner. Twice a year, she'd visit New York and together we would see four shows in three days.

Once we entered the twenty-first century, our email exchanges — based on a lifetime of shared experiences — were screamingly funny, at least to each other (c.f. her email in *Hillsdale Journal*). Brooke and I both longed to devote more time to personal writing and, in August of 1997, she called to say she had signed us up for Nightwriters, a creative writing seminar in Tuscany that fall. The leader was Phyllis Theroux, a gifted essayist, columnist, author, and teacher, whose work was published in national magazines and newspapers. The subject matter was our personal lives.

I felt guilty telling anyone that I was going to Italy to write about myself. The week sounded like an unjustifiable exercise in narcissism. But the workshop was magical. Words poured out of me, and I was hooked. Brook wrote on her laptop, and I filled notebook after notebook in longhand (a word that sounds antiquated now). I couldn't write fast enough. When my hand began to cramp, I had to force myself to let go of my ballpoint pen.

Over the eight days, I wrote sixty pages, most about my daughter's childhood bout with Stage IV Hodgkin's disease, almost ten years earlier, something neither she or I ever talked about. But by writing about the most terrifying two years of my life, I was finally able to free myself of the unexpressed fear I'd carried since the day she was diagnosed. As I read those pages aloud, I felt as if my shoulders dropped about two inches and I could finally breathe.

I'd found an effective escape valve for feelings I'd buried for years. And it was comforting and energizing to share those feelings with fellow writers who responded to my stories with empathy and support. The week was all about connecting.

I returned to New York full of good intentions: to keep a daily journal, to write essays, to continue taking workshops; but again, life intervened. I got married for the second time. My husband

and I bought a country house and two English Spaniel puppies. In addition to my daughter and her future husband living with us, I also now had two (part-time) teenage stepchildren.

A few years slipped by. Then, after ten years in remission, my husband's cancer returned and a year later, he died. I sold the house in the country, I continued to run my business, and went back and forth to Europe, visiting my wine clients. I was writing every day but, once again, never about myself.

Then came *The Prednisone Princess Diaries.* In 2011, two years after my mother passed away, I discovered a stubborn little white bump on my right leg, two inches above the knee. The bump wouldn't go away. When I finally got to the right doctor, he correctly diagnosed it as Stage IV melanoma. I was fortunate: not only do I live six blocks from Memorial Sloan Kettering, one of the best cancer hospitals in the world, but I also had immediate access to the doctor at the forefront of melanoma research and treatment.

My doctor told me that most patients who present with Stage IV melanoma have six months. But, due to the number of cutting-edge drugs — many developed by my doctor and his team at MSK — here I am, seven years later, madly tapping away at my keyboard.

Another reason that MSK is such a terrific hospital is because it treats the whole patient — not just the cancer. In addition to immunotherapy, surgery, radiation, and targeted therapy, they also offer psychotherapy, acupuncture, massage, yoga, and nutritional counseling, all of which I tried, with varied degrees of success.

But best of all, they offer *Visible Ink*, a writing program open to all patients, "to promote creativity, stress reduction and personal empowerment for people diagnosed with cancer." The program pairs patients with a writing mentor and, in my first year, my essay, *The Prednisone Princess Diaries*, was chosen from hundreds of submissions for the Visible Ink anthology and the stage performance. It was a thrill to hear my words come alive, read by a professional actress. I was astounded by the laughter and had to restrain myself from standing up mid-performance to motion the actress to *slow down*, since the audience's laughter was drowning out the lines.

Since then, I have submitted pieces to *Visible Ink* and every year one of my essays is selected for their anthology. Although they touch on my experience with illness, readers are often surprised to find them funny. My friend Ralph came up with a great name for these writings, *Sick Humor*, which I've borrowed for Section VII of this book.

The response made me realize that humor was the filter through which I have always viewed my life, and that it is not only a powerful coping mechanism, but also a great connector. So this has become my mission: to connect with as many people as possible, knowing that humor can shine a light on even the darkest corners.

This winter, I decided to take a writers' workshop with Judi Hannan, my *Visible Ink* mentor. This workshop met at Shakespeare & Co., the neighborhood bookstore a block and a half from my house. How could I resist?

After twenty-three years of running the wine and spirits marketing company, The Dunn-Robbins Group, most with my partner, Brian Dunn, I had closed my office in the Flatiron

District, and now worked from home. Aside from spending time with my granddaughter, Sage, a major commitment to *Les Dames d'Escoffier*, and a few consulting jobs, I now had time to write.

Judi created a safe welcoming space through weekly writing prompts and in-class exercises. As I grew more comfortable with the class, my pieces became more honest, more revealing, and funnier. When I read them aloud, the women around the table were genuinely laughing. One insisted I should do stand-up and I told her I already had.

For my last class in Judi's workshop, the prompt was to "Write about an inanimate object that knows you very well, and could describe your life, inside and out." I wrote my essay from the point of view of my bedroom closet.

Right after the class had started, a pretty blonde woman wandered in off the street, having seen a workshop flyer in the bookstore's front window. Not knowing it was a formal eight-week class, she descended the rickety stairs to the bookstore's basement, where she found six women sitting around a rectangular oak table. She asked if she might join us, and Judi explained that we were finishing the semester but she was welcome to join us that night.

This woman, Constance, sat down next to me. Through her insightful comments on the stories we read aloud, I could tell that she was a writer and editor. When asked, she admitted that I was correct.

I read the closet piece aloud, which brought on gales of laughter. After class, Constance and I chatted. She had been a professional journalist and book coach. I asked her where she had learned her writing and editing skills, and she said, "With someone whose workshop changed my life, and with whom I worked for several years."

"Who was that?" I asked.

"Phyllis Theroux," she answered.

I practically fell off my chair.

We discovered that she had attended the workshop in Tuscany the week before I had. She had been living in Virginia, had worked with Phyllis, and had just moved to New York a few months ago. But our paths were not fated to cross until that evening, twenty years later, in the basement of a small bookstore in New York City. She spoke enthusiastically about my reading and told me that I should be performing these for a much larger audience.

"I'd love to, but I have no idea how to reach them," I said.

"I can help," she said.

A week later, Constance was sitting across from me at my kitchen table, helping to outline a personal memoir, comprised of my favorite essays.

One of her questions was, "What was the impact of being diagnosed with Stage IV melanoma?"

"It made me realize that there's no time for small talk," I responded off the top of my head.

"That's it!" she said excitedly, "That's your title." And so, it is.

January 2019

no time
for small talk

I

Eat, Shop, Sing

One of the very nicest things about life is the way we must regularly stop whatever it is we are doing and devote our attention to eating.

~ Luciano Pavarotti

Anyone who lives within their means suffers from a lack of imagination.

~ Oscar Wilde

Food as Raison d'Être

MY PARENTS WERE EPICURES of a fairly high order. They reinforced my interest and pleasure in meals from the time I was old enough to chew. So naturally, I define myself through food. And it surprised no one when I ended up running my own wine and food company for twenty-four years.

My earliest and most vivid food memory was the celebration of my sixth birthday, when my parents took my sister and me to The Stork Club, a former speakeasy and chic night spot on East 53rd Street. Unprompted, I ordered sautéed frog legs. Not only were they sized perfectly for a child's fingers, they were also totally delicious. It didn't bother me that they looked exactly like the bottom half of a frog. They were sautéed in butter and garlic with a squeeze of fresh lemon and a sprinkling of fresh bright green parsley. When I was older, I realized that they probably also had been dusted lightly with flour to form a golden crust, which would absorb more of the butter and garlic. The waiter looked a bit taken aback when I announced my choice of entrée, but my parents beamed. It became one of their favorite stories about their budding gastronome.

My father, always an adventurous eater, loved introducing us to new cuisines, from street foods to Chinese banquet halls to fancy French restaurants. He had many old favorites, too, including Katz's on the Lower East Side, Peter Luger's in Brooklyn, Barney Greengrass on the Upper West Side, as well as Lutèce and the Four Seasons. But his all-time favorite was Romeo Salta's, a high-end Italian restaurant on West 56th Street, where we celebrated all our family's special occasions.

In Romeo's obituary, the *New York Times* referred to him as "one of the first in Manhattan to offer elegant Northern Italian cooking." Upon his death, Mimi Sheraton, former *Times* restaurant critic, said "New York has never had an Italian restaurant as good as Romeo Salta was in its heyday." It was truly ground-breaking. In the late '50s, most Italian restaurants were still serving spaghetti and meatballs with red sauce on a red checked tablecloth with a candle-stuffed straw Chianti bottle on the table. In dramatic contrast to these "red sauce joints" which pandered to American tastes, Romeo served authentic Italian cuisine with imported ingredients, many prepared tableside. I still remember the tender, pounded-thin slices of lemony veal piccata in a light stock and white wine sauce with capers; melt-in-your-mouth *paglia e fieno* (yellow egg pasta and green spinach pasta in a light cream sauce with peas and prosciutto with a dusting of freshly grated Parmesan), and the lightest but profoundly satisfying spinach lasagna. He also introduced several dishes which are taken for granted today: gnocchi, scampi, and risotto.

My father, who happened to be Romeo's lawyer, also became one of his close friends, and one summer, Romeo invited our family to spend a week with him and his family in their summer home outside Florence.

I was eleven years old when we spent that week in Italy, but there was one meal that has stayed fresh in my mind. Romeo took my family and several members of his extended family to a small restaurant, about an hour away, deep in the country. The owners had set up one big table on their patio, partially shaded by a grape arbor, overlooking a beautiful valley. The lunch started at around one in the afternoon and lasted until six that evening. It wasn't that we ate constantly for four hours; there were pauses between the many courses (hot and cold antipasti, pasta, fish, meat, salad, cheese, and desserts, accompanied by a number of different wines), but there was an endless flow of conversation and of wine, so the meal expanded to fill the entire afternoon.

While the grown-ups talked and ate and drank, the kids occasionally were excused from the table and ran or rolled down the hill or just lay in the grass and looked up at the clouds. The main wine was a local *Verdicchio*, and the party must have gone through at least six bottles. I remember my parents trying to find it once they returned to New York, but they couldn't. I understood when I was older that part of its deliciousness was linked with the place, the time of day, the sunlight, the air, the fresh local ingredients, and the company.

Back in New York, my father continued to take us to wonderful restaurants. A few years later, when I was in high school and beginning to be asked out on dates, my father admitted that one of the reasons that he was taking my sister and me to fancy restaurants, was so that we would never be impressed by any young man who took us to such restaurants, in an effort to seduce us.

This did not have the desired effect, however. First of all, it set the bar very high. Very few of the young men I met had an equal appreciation of really good food, no less a history of fine dining experiences. And second of all, I found I had developed very expensive taste in restaurants, so any young man who really wanted to impress me practically had to fly me to Paris to eat at *La Tour d'Argent.*

My passion for food made me into a curious and adventurous cook. This was especially true when I was first married and trying much too hard to impress my husband, his friends, and clients. I became a fanatic: I made my own stocks, roasted my own hazelnuts, made pasta from scratch, ground my own coffee beans (I drew the line at roasting them), made my own gelato. I even took a Chinese cooking course and ended up co-authoring a book with the teacher, Karen Lee. Our book, *Chinese Cooking for the American Kitchen* was nominated for a James Beard Award.

There was one meal I made during the second year of my marriage that stands out. It was a dinner party that I prepared for my husband's boring and basically unappreciative clients. I kept notes in a Dinner Diary, a red leather-bound blank book which my friends Pat and Ralph had given me. On the left-hand page were columns for the different courses and wines, while the right-hand page contained an oval representing the dinner table, where I filled in the seating plan. This particular client dinner took place on May 18, 1977. I served oysters on the half shelf with a mignonette sauce as an appetizer in the living room. When we moved to the dining room, the plated entrée was *noisettes d'agneau* on fresh artichoke bottoms with a Madeira sauce, accompanied by oven-roasted potatoes, *haricots verts*, and salsify. Then I dashed into the kitchen to whip up an *intermezzo* of Campari-Grapefruit Sorbet, to clear the palate. This was followed by a cheese course with apricot mostarda and almond-raisin toasts. Dessert was a chocolate raspberry cake accompanied by assorted meringue drops.

At the end of the meal, as I was scraping plates before putting them in the dishwasher, I felt my shoulders and neck begin to cramp and spasm. I was so tired I started to cry. I decided that was the last formal dinner party I would give. It was emblematic of the issues in my marriage itself, all of which I chose to ignore for a number of years.

I was finally divorced in 1982, with a three-year old daughter to raise. I worked as a journalist, and then joined a PR firm. One of their clients was Campari USA and, after six months, Campari hired me to serve as their in-house Director of Communications. Huge perk: I ate superb Italian meals accompanied by great Italian wines (some of which we were beginning to import), not only in NYC, but on our trips to Milan.

Then in 1994, I started my own marketing and strategic company with a partner, Brian Dunn. This was a wonderful job — I wrote about wines, gave lectures about wines to consumers and trade; created menus, pairing wines with food, and took journalists to visit wineries in the different countries that we represented. Over a twenty-year period, I got to visit wineries, drink magnificent wines, and eat the local foods in some of the world's greatest wine regions in Spain, Italy, Portugal, Argentina, Israel, and South Africa.

Then my food world — my entire life — suddenly collapsed. To surgically remove malignancies in my abdomen, I had to undergo an intestinal resection. The procedure was successful but I developed an obstruction. After two weeks in the hospital, I was released.

I had to go back to eating gradually. Talk about cruel and unusual punishment. For about six months, I couldn't eat dairy, gluten, meat, raw fruits and vegetables, or cooked cruciferous vegetables, nothing spicy, and no alcohol.

Having been forced to give up all food and drink for that two-week period, when I finally could add back most of the major food groups, I found myself deriving enormous pleasure from each and every piece of delicious food and every sip of a delicious beverage that I put in my mouth. In fact, if each meal didn't include something truly delicious, I got upset; it was a missed opportunity. It didn't have to be fancy, it just had to be delicious. It could be an omelet, a pasta, a Pavlova, or even a square of dark chocolate.

The other night, I went to *Il Buco Alimentari e Vineria* on Great Jones Street. I ordered a homemade farro pasta which was so delicious, it reminded me of the luncheon on the hill under the grape arbor. And although I try to make it myself at home, I've never eaten a veal piccata as good as Romeo's.

October 2017

VEAL PICCATA: RECIPE

Tender veal scaloppini dredged in flour and sautéed in butter gets a boost of brightness from a simple pan sauce made with white wine and a generous squeeze of lemon.

Ingredients

- 2 lb. (about 12) veal cutlets (scaloppini) pounded until 1/4" thick
- Kosher salt and freshly ground black pepper, to taste
- 1/2 cup flour
- 4 tbsp. unsalted butter
- 2 tbsp. olive oil
- 1/2 cup dry white wine
- 1 1/4 cups chicken stock
- 1 lemon, thinly sliced
- 1 tbsp. fresh lemon juice
- 1/4 cup capers, drained
- 2 tbsp. chopped parsley

Instructions

1. Season veal with salt and pepper and dredge in flour, shaking off excess.
2. Heat 2 tbsp. butter and oil in a 12" skillet over medium-high heat. Working in batches, add veal, and cook, turning once, until golden brown, about 3 minutes. Transfer to a serving platter, and set aside.
3. Add wine to skillet, and cook, scraping bottom of pan until reduced by half, about 3 minutes. Add stock and lemon slices, and bring to a boil; cook until reduced by half, about 8 minutes.

4. Add remaining butter, juice, capers, and parsley, and season with salt and pepper.
5. Pour sauce over veal and serve immediately.

Note: *If uncooked cutlets are more than 1/4-inch-thick, pound to 1/4 inch thick between 2 sheets of plastic wrap with a rolling pin.*

The Retail Gene

I WAS LUCKY TO know my great-grandmother, Rose, who lived until I was twelve. She was Rose Zarinsky before she married my great-grandfather, Max Zeitz. Both were born in New York City and together they founded and ran a small Brooklyn department store that carried high-quality merchandise. Rose was an elegant woman who moved into the Schwab House on 72nd Street and Riverside Drive in the 1950s. She always wore powder, rouge, and lipstick and, in photographs, she would tilt her chin up to elongate her neck or wrap her hand around her neck so no one would see the wrinkles.

Of Rose's five children — three boys and two girls — only one, Isabel, the second oldest, inherited the fashion gene. Her parents were disappointed when Isabel fell in love with Sam Elowsky and married him. Sam was first generation and had dropped out of high school at fifteen to help his Russian immigrant parents run their mom-and-pop grocery store in Brooklyn.

Isabel's parents thought she was "marrying beneath her," but Sam was a brilliant, hardworking entrepreneur who became an extremely successful wholesale manufacturer of women's sportswear. He was able to provide a luxurious lifestyle for his wife, far beyond that of her parents.

By the '70s, Sam owned five different manufacturing companies. He sold his products in mind-boggling quantities to national department stores such as JC Penney. I worked for him one summer and was staggered by the size of the orders and what a brilliant negotiator he was, arguing for two cents more per dozen — and getting it. He could multiply a twelve-digit number by another twelve-digit number in his head in seconds. He had a large office in the heart of the garment district at 1147 Broadway, with factories located in Herkimer, NY and Moonachie, NJ. Throughout his life he remained a quiet, modest man, who gave jobs to his own and his wife's relatives.

When my mother, Mildred, who was Isabel's daughter, married Louis J. Robbins in 1940, everyone lived in Brooklyn, which was a far cry from the hipster playground it is today. My upwardly-mobile father thought it was important to move into Manhattan, however. So, before they were married, he found an apartment on Sutton Place for himself and his new bride. My father also wanted his in-laws to move into Manhattan; not only for prestige, but because it would be so much easier for my grandfather to get to work (he traveled by subway).

At my father's urging, my grandparents sold their brownstone in Brooklyn. He moved them into a residential suite at the Hotel St. Moritz, on the corner of Central Park South and Sixth

Avenue. The twenty-ninth floor apartment was stunning, with a bedroom, a den, a small kitchen, and a living room with French doors that opened onto a terrace overlooking Central Park. The view alone was spectacular, changing with each season. But neither the view nor the elegance were what won over Grandma Isabel.

"Oh, Lou!" she exclaimed when they went to visit the suite. "It's perfect—I fall out of bed and I'm in Bergdorf's!" That did it. Although my father showed them a number of other apartments with wonderful addresses and beautiful views, Grandma could not be budged. She and Sam would go on to live there for forty-seven years.

Isabell and Sam as young marrieds.

Truth be told, however, the St. Moritz had another strong selling point: the old-fashioned ice cream parlor, Rumpelmayer's, built when the hotel was first constructed, in 1930. Although the restaurant itself was beautiful, modeled in the Art Deco Style after the Rumpelmayer's in Paris from the early 1900s, what Grandma Isabel really loved was that she could order up sundaes on room service.

That would be her entire lunch, about three times a week. Although Grandpa Sam was a bit of a health nut, eating mostly salads, fish, steamed vegetables, and steady handfuls of nuts, nothing green ever passed her lips. Rumpelmayer's offered the perfect food as far as she was concerned. Although it didn't offer HoJo's twenty-eight flavors, it was the crème de la crème of dessert emporiums. The French ice cream was house-made, as were all the toppings. The sundaes were served in silver coupes and the hot sauces (fudge and butterscotch) were served on the side in little ceramic pitchers, so they didn't melt the ice cream before it arrived at the table or, in Grandma's case, before it was brought up to her apartment. Toppings included candied walnuts, crushed pineapple, strawberries, and one of her favorites: marshmallow. Plus, there was always fresh whipped cream on top. She would often mix a few toppings, such as butterscotch, walnut, and marshmallow.

Considering the only exercise she got was shopping, Isabel was never svelte. But she dressed in such tasteful and elegant clothes that you never noticed she was not a model size six. Her diet was a far cry from healthy, but the woman was only hospitalized at the births of her two children and she lived to eighty-seven.

Once she moved into the St. Moritz, her career as a world-class shopper blossomed. She had two favorite stores: Bergdorf Goodman's and Saks; and she had personal shoppers at both. She occasionally took me with her, introducing me to a world that bedazzled me. At the start of each new couture season, she would set up appointments with her personal shoppers. The woman at Bergdorf's or Saks would lead her into the largest fitting room where ensembles hung on all the walls, on pegs and bars. At Bergdorf's, the evening gowns, suits, dresses, and coats were mostly by the American haute couture designer, Norman Norell. Born in the year 1900, Grandma Isabel never wore pants. The idea of women wearing them remained a bit shocking to her.

Grandma would try almost everything on, since the saleswomen knew her taste, then evaluate herself mercilessly in the three-way mirror. And since she was not a perfect size, the saleswoman then called for the seamstress. At both stores, Grandma also knew these women well. She took a personal interest in both them and the saleswomen, always asking about their families, remembering what their children were studying, where they were working, if they were married. And every Christmas, she gave them elbow-length cashmere gloves.

After an exhausting morning trying on clothes, Grandma would head directly to the luncheon café in Bergdorf's, which served a variety of little crust-less sandwiches on white bread: lobster salad, crab salad, shrimp salad, egg salad. This was all the more delicious since she could never eat any of these foods at home; her husband was Kosher, having grown up in an

Orthodox home. If, for a change of pace, she went to Schrafft's, she always ordered a BLT.

Grandma Isabel had excellent taste and an ability to put ensembles together with creativity and class. I remember that the night before any social occasion or event, whether it was a fitting in a department store, dinner with friends, the theatre, or the high holidays at Fifth Avenue Synagogue — which Grandpa Sam had helped found — she would choose and lay out her outfit. This started with the dress, undergarments, including a heavy-duty girdle, stockings, pumps, a pocketbook with an embroidered personalized handkerchief doused in her signature perfume, Bellodgia (introduced by Caron in 1927); earrings, a brooch, double or triple strand of pearls, rings, gloves, and a hat.

Grandma's passion for fashion did not extend to her pretty, dark-eyed, raven-haired daughter, Mildred. My mother, who went by Millie, had been dressed to the nines as a child. In many photographs, she sports a huge bow which is practically the size of her head.

Once she was a teenager, though, Millie rebelled against what she considered to be Grandma's superficial values and refused to shop. This continued throughout her adult life. She would purchase items from catalogs or, if she were going down Fifth Avenue on a bus and saw an item in a department store window, she would call and order it in her size, delivered.

Millie's arguments with her mother about appearance didn't stop at clothes. Isabel had a weekly manicure for her entire life, but nail polish never touched my mother's fingers or toes. And the subject of hair color only escalated tensions. Most of the women on that side of the family, Great-Grandma Rose,

Grandma Isabel, my mother, and I all went prematurely grey. As soon as Isabel saw a few grey hairs in her mid-twenties, she immediately set up an appointment at the beauty salon and, for the rest of her life, she had her hair colored every three weeks. Never tempted to become a blonde, she maintained her natural brunette color.

My mother, of course, refused to dye her hair. She had married at eighteen, ostensibly to get out of the house because her father objected to her subscribing to what he considered a Communist rag, *The New Republic*. She did have leftist leanings and she had done volunteer work for liberal organizations from the time she was married. In each case, she always rose to the top, so she liked her grey hair, since it made her look older and gave her a certain gravitas.

So, the retail gene skipped my mother, but came to full flower in me.

When I was sixteen, Grandma Isabel decided to take me shopping for a fall wardrobe. She took me to Saks, where her saleswoman had recommended someone in a more appropriate department for a teenager. It was the same drill. Grandma would make an appointment and when we showed up our personal shopper would have already brought outfits into the fitting room; but this time, for me.

My taste was not fully formed at that age, so I let Grandma Isabel make the final selection. So much attention lavished on me! So many beautiful new outfits! I felt spoiled and not a little guilty. She gave me important beauty and fashion tips, such as, "Make sure you always look perfect from the waist up. That's what the person sitting across the table from you at dinner sees."

And, "constantly re-apply lipstick." And, "find a signature fragrance." My mother never wore perfume, claiming it made her sneeze.

Grandma took me on the fall shopping spree for the next two years. But once I went away to college in California during the turbulent '60s, my mode of dressing had to change drastically. I went for protective camouflage and affected a hippie look: bell bottom jeans, tie-dyed T-shirts, feather earrings, leather vests, sandals.

This all came to a dead halt when, two years after I graduated from college, I announced my engagement to someone who, at least outwardly, seemed to be an appropriate match. He came from a good family, had gone to the right schools, and cared greatly about appearances.

I was the first of her grandchildren to marry, so my grandmother was in heaven at the thought of shopping for my wedding dress and trousseau. Predictably, her only daughter, Millie, had refused to wear the traditional long white wedding gown at her wedding. She wore a pale green suit with a knee-length skirt and instead of a bouquet, carried branches of quince. The only traditional touch was a hat with a long veil.

My mother was present when I was trying on wedding gowns, but it was Grandma Isabel and I who made the final decisions about the gown, the veil, the shoes, the jewelry, the hairstyle, and the flowers. Every night, we would speak on the phone about what pieces were still missing from my trousseau.

I have a beautiful photo of her and Grandpa Sam, dancing at my wedding. And an even more wonderful photo of them with Ariel, my daughter, who was born a year before Grandpa Sam died.

A year later, Grandma died. She never recovered from the death of her beloved husband of sixty-one years. At the time, I was a young mother with a toddler, working part-time while attending graduate school. I was soon to be divorced, so I wasn't spending money on clothes. Occasionally, I would wander into an expensive boutique when a big sale was going on, but mostly I bought pieces based on what a great bargain I was getting, not because the clothes were particularly flattering. I hadn't seen the saleswoman in Saks for over a decade. I was sure she had retired.

Things changed in the mid-'90s, when I started my own company with a partner and began to make a decent living. My days were filled with client meetings and presentations, so I had to look well put-together at all times. With this in mind, I started checking out some of the boutiques and high-end department stores again.

Gradually, I made friends with some key salespeople — Vincenzo at the Giorgio Armani flagship store on Madison, Robyn at the Max Mara boutique, and Carmela on the couture floor of Saks. In fact, I became good friends with Carmela. She called me when she had outfits she wanted me to try on, and emailed me photos. I was so impressed by her attention and taste that I wrote the following letter to her supervisor at Saks:

June 6, 2012 : *A letter of commendation for Carmela Guariscio*

Every time I have shopped with Carmela, she has devoted a number of hours to me, and I never felt as if her attention was divided. Quite to the contrary; if she were not in the fitting room, then she was dashing all over the store, looking for different pieces in different colors, shapes and sizes. She is indefatigable and enthusiastic.

I should mention that I am an inveterate shopper, with long-standing relationships with sales people in several couture boutiques (no one ever in Saks, however), but Carmela has set the bar higher than ever.
She is honest, and will tell me whether something really looks good or not; she never pressures me to buy, and respects my own judgment. Although she is a consummate professional, she makes it feel as if I am shopping with a girlfriend who just so happens to have a profound knowledge of fashion. She was even able to identify the dress that Katie Couric wore on the Queen's Jubilee special broadcast (Max Mara).

Do whatever you can to keep her; she upgrades the service and the image of your iconic store.

Sincerely,
Aileen Robbins

This letter was read aloud at a staff meeting. Everyone applauded. Carmela was so touched at my having taken the time to write such a positive review to her boss that she sent me a beautiful gold bowl by Michael Aram.

My true nature as a compulsive shopper has finally been allowed to come out, even though I try to stay within a budget. Sometimes, I must admit, I shop for the wrong reasons. I can barely wedge one more hanger in any of my closets or shoehorn another sweater into my drawer. But when I have spent too many hours alone working on my computer and need to interact with people and purchases, shopping fills a void. It's a little like compulsive eating although, with shopping, when I suffer from buyer's remorse, I spend a good deal of time returning items. I figure this is better than bulimia.

Now we come to the next generation. When my daughter, Ariel, was growing up, I was able to keep my compulsive shopping pretty much under control. So she didn't rebel against it, like my mother did against her mother's.

Unlike Grandma Isabel and me, however, Ariel doesn't like to shop. In fact, she is the direct opposite of an impulse shopper. She will see something, think about it for a few days, then maybe go back and buy it. If it's there, fine, if not, she figures she wasn't meant to have it. (I still regret not getting the white suit at Hermès, which I tried on six years ago.) She shops online, checking out eBay, Etsy, and other retail sites. We have such radically different taste that I can never buy anything for her, not even a simple gold necklace.

But there's a twist. To my surprise and delight, from her early teens, Ariel was focused on a career in retail. Every summer, and sometimes over Christmas vacation, she worked in a store — Ralph Lauren in East Hampton and Lilly Pulitzer in Nantucket — and when she graduated from college, she went directly into the management course at Saks. After Saks, she was at Bendel's.

She was always very good at her job and now she's the Senior Director of Merchandising for Kate Spade. So although she has Grandma Isabel's sense of composition, color and balance, she also has Grandpa Sam's administrative and management skills.

She throws together an Excel document like I throw together a recipe.

It makes me wish that Grandpa Sam and Grandma Isabel could see her now.

They would both be so proud.

February 2017

The Gift of Song

I WAS SIX YEARS old when I was sent to a two-month summer sleep-away camp in Vermont called Sky Hollow Farm. At that age, I suppose I should have been homesick but, for two reasons, I wasn't. First, the farm was surrounded by balsam pine, whose fallen needles smelled so delicious that I could almost taste them. And second, on most nights after dinner we sat around a campfire and, while a counselor played guitar, we sang folk songs.

I knew most of the songs by heart because, at home, my older sister Jane and I listened endlessly to folk albums. We'd played our 33s of the Weavers, Pete Seeger, and Woody Guthrie so many times that I'd memorized both the melodies and the harmonies. Our small circle of Sky Hollow girls welcomed the warmth of the big fire as it spit and crackled, setting off sparks. And I joined in wholeheartedly as we sang, often starting with the melody but then shifting into harmony, sliding up or down a fifth, a third, or sometimes a second resolving into a third.

One night, about a week into the summer, the guitar-playing

counselor came over to me at the end of the sing-along. "Where did you learn how to do that?" she asked.

"Do what?" I answered.

"Sing the different lines of harmony."

"I've heard the different voices on records. My sister and I play those songs all the time," I admitted, thinking maybe I was in trouble. "Is that cheating? Am I not supposed to do that?"

"Oh no, you're not cheating," said the counselor, "you're *improvising*. You have a good ear, and a good sense of relative pitch, which means you can both carry a tune and harmonize with it. I've rarely heard a six-year-old who can do that."

I wasn't sure what she meant by *a good ear* or *relative pitch* but her words were encouraging and I looked forward to those campfire sing-alongs more than ever. With the firelight barely illuminating our faces in the darkness, I felt like an instrument; my disembodied voice connecting to and blending with the other voices. The sound of our music created a magic circle, enclosing us in a safe space that felt familiar and comforting. I couldn't have described this out-of-body experience at the time, but I would recognize it when it happened again when I was older.

I come from a musical family. Whenever we got together with my mother's side of the family, my Uncle Larry, a jazz pianist and songwriter, would play the piano after dinner while we gathered around him to sing. Although my mother played piano, and my grandmother could sight-read sheet music while singing in her beautiful sweet high voice, Uncle Larry was the true musician in the family. By his twenties, he had memorized around 300 songs from the Great American Songbook. We kept the sheet music on the piano just so everyone could read the lyrics during these sing-alongs.

I used to stand on Uncle Larry's right, the prime spot to watch his hands glide over the keys. He could automatically transpose a song to another key and he never looked down; his fingers just knew where to find the notes. Someone would call out a favorite song, and we'd sing through dozens of them. When I was older and studying voice, Uncle Larry would play songs just for me to sing, solo. My grandfather, a fan of both opera and the American songbook, would sit in a corner and beam, as would my father, a former violinist.

I kept singing throughout middle and high school; in musical theatre, in a madrigal group, and in the school chorus. In my senior year, my school choir was chosen to join choirs from several other New York City schools to sing Debussy's third Nocturne, *Sirènes*, at Carnegie Hall. Just standing on that stage, flooded with bright lights, in a packed hall where I'd heard some of the great artists of the day perform, was magical. *Sirènes* is an otherworldly vocalise, a wordless piece written for women's voices, accompanied mostly by woodwinds and harps. The fatal seductive song of the Sirens themselves was blended with the impressionistic sounds of waves and wind.

As we began to sing, I felt my feet lose contact with the stage, and I began to float. It was the strongest out-of-body experience I had ever had, brought on through the medium of sound, both the sound that I myself produced as well as the sounds all around me. I felt like a drop in an ocean of sound.

That night I decided that I was going to be a singer.

A few weeks later I auditioned for the Aspen Music School's

summer opera program. I was accepted and spent two months studying with Madame Olga Ryss, one of the leading opera teachers of the day. Learning operatic technique was hard work, I discovered. Rather than leaving my body, I had to enter it. I had to learn and build breath control, stamina, concentration, and repeat scales, arpeggios, and coloratura exercises endlessly. Madame Ryss was a large and totally terrifying Russian woman with grey braids that looped around her head. At some point during almost every lesson in the first few weeks, she would bang on the piano keys with both fists and shriek at the top of her lungs, "That's enough! I can't listen to this any more, your lesson is over." I would fight back tears but, before they spilled down my cheeks, she would say in a hoarse stage whisper, *"but come back on Thursday."*

By the end of the summer, Madame Ryss said I should consider going to Juilliard to continue vocal studies. I had already accepted a place at Stanford University, but a career as an opera singer was tempting. When I returned home, I discussed this possibility with my parents and we scheduled a meeting with Madame Ryss at her apartment on West 77th Street.

"Your daughter has a definite talent which could be developed," she said.

"I agree," said my father, "a beautiful voice is a gift and it's her responsibility to share that gift." Those were words he had never said to me, words I never forgot.

Madame Ryss went on in her stern heavily-Russian accented English, "But you have to understand from the start that *singing is a disease!* It takes tremendous dedication and discipline. It will eclipse everything in your daughter's life — friends, marriage, children — it would be her only focus for many years. Is she ready to make that sacrifice?"

That was the biggest and scariest decision I had ever had to make, one which would affect my entire life. My parents and I thanked Madame Ryss for her candor and said we'd think it over. By the time we reached home, fifteen minutes later, we'd all reached the same conclusion, rare for a teenager and her parents: I should pursue my liberal arts degree and participate in musical performances while at college. And so, I did — opera, musical theatre, folk, jazz.

When I graduated from college, I returned to New York and resumed serious voice lessons with Rose Bampton, an opera singer had enjoyed a long and brilliant career at the Metropolitan Opera and was now teaching at Juilliard. In addition to weekly voice lessons, I worked with a music coach; brushed up on my French, Italian, and German; listened to innumerable recordings, attended a vast number of operas and concerts, and read primary commentary on the cultural and historical context of the composers and librettists. At the same time, I entered the Ph.D. program in Dramatic Literature at New York University.

Over the next few years, I finished my doctoral courses, passed my oral and written exams, and researched a dissertation on Otto Kahn. To support myself, I worked first as Managing Editor of *The Drama Review* and then as an Editor at The Drama Bookshop. During that time, I also broke two of Madame Ryss' cardinal rules: I got married and had a child. As she had predicted, it grew increasingly difficult to balance singing with working, motherhood, and marriage. Something had to give and what gave was my marriage. Suddenly, I was a single working mother with a three-year-old daughter.

But I continued auditioning and performing with workshops and opera companies, unwilling to give up what I had worked ten years to achieve. My efforts paid off, culminating in a Main Stage audition with Beverly Sills at New York City Opera. My accompanist, Ruth Bierhoff, and I were alone on what was then the New York State Theatre stage at Lincoln Center.

I positioned myself in the crook of the grand piano and started to sing, amazed at how my voice expanded to fill that cavernous space. It was as if all the lessons and hours of practice kicked in and I felt the column of air which so many voice teachers prattle on about, supporting the sound so it flowed out and reached the highest rows in the last balcony. It was hard to believe that big voice was my own.

"You have talent and intelligence but you don't have enough experience," said Sills at the end of the audition. "You need to go to Germany and sing key roles in some of the small opera houses. When you return, I'll hear you again. I have roles in mind for you."

She was right. I didn't have much experience with professional opera companies, no less international houses. But while I reveled in the joy of the audition and her praise, I was unwilling to move to Germany with a toddler, to sing in small German opera houses for who-knew how many years. I had one child and my chances of having more were not great. There was no contest. My audition on the stage of New York City Opera was my last performance.

The decision was easy, but ending my singing career wasn't.

My voice was my instrument, my way of engaging with other people. Now, not-singing meant eradicating an identity I'd spent a decade building. For over a year, I couldn't walk by Carnegie Hall or Lincoln Center, couldn't listen to the classical radio station, couldn't go to friends' recitals or the Metropolitan Opera, without grief constricting my chest, causing a lump to rise in my throat.

Singing was a way of releasing energy and emotion, a primal sound that echoed in my head, in my chest, and throughout the room as well as my body. Singing was a way of expressing joy and sorrow, as my first voice teacher had explained, "when spoken words were not enough." And most importantly, it was a way to connect those feelings with the feelings of the people listening.

It was a difficult adjustment but I have no regrets. I was working part-time, which allowed me more time with my daughter. I loved taking her to school and gymnastics and play dates, which my own mother had been quick to delegate to our housekeeper. I loved helping with homework and supervising art projects, even if it meant glitter on the kitchen table and floor for days. I loved having her friends spend the night and loved that they all wanted to come over to our house.

In time, I began to feel relief. I no longer had to drink endless cups of hot lemon tea with honey and ginger to stay hydrated. I no longer sat with a towel over my head, inhaling steam from a bowl of boiling water mixed with tincture of Benzoin to moisturize my cords. There were no more pre-audition or pre-performance nights when I couldn't eat dairy, couldn't drink alcohol, and couldn't go to any restaurant or party where anyone was smoking or I had to speak loudly. The only habit I maintained was wrapping a scarf around my neck, no matter what the season. After a few years, I was even able to listen to WQXR and attend operas and recitals without feeling my heart constrict.

Then one spring, the singing disease, which had lay dormant for almost twenty years, flared up. I sat in on an inspiring Opera Master Class given by my best friend Peter, an opera singer, director, and teacher who has performed in major opera houses all over the world. As I listened to his students, all of whom had very good voices, I heard talent and technique, but they were so young that they had no life experience, and couldn't bring much to the characters that they were portraying. I complimented Peter afterwards. He'd done wonders with these puppies, and I expressed sincere admiration for his work but, having spent the past twenty years gathering a range of life experiences, I added that I could interpret those songs and arias better than they could.

"Of course you can," he said.

As soon as I returned to New York, I started taking voice lessons again. My voice was rusty, and I was very out of shape — singing opera is like running a marathon — but I practiced every day, and slowly, over a period of months, the breath, the stamina and even some of the high notes and vocal flexibility started coming back.

One summer afternoon, I was taken to a friend-of-a-friend's house for a holiday party. Phil, the host, was a successful lawyer, who also happened to be a talented pianist. That afternoon, he played selections from the Great American Songbook. Guests drifted by the piano to sing an occasional line or chorus. When he got to George & Ira Gershwin's song, *But Not for Me*, though, I couldn't stand it for another minute. I positioned myself on Phil's right, where I could glance at the words, and sang every note straight from the heart.

The room grew quiet. Heads turned our way. Everyone was listening. When Phil and I finished, there was a spontaneous round of applause.

"You're a singer!" exclaimed Phil.

"I used to be," I responded, ruefully.

"No, you're still a singer," said Phil. There were murmurs of agreement around the room.

"Well, these songs barely cover an octave; they're easy to sing," I said. "I used to sing opera. But I've always loved the Great American Songbook."

Phil and I read through several more songs. I was singing at half voice, since I didn't want to call too much attention to myself — the old singer's neurosis surfacing — I hadn't warmed up properly.

"It's great to accompany you," said Phil. "I think we should give a concert."

Without a moment's pause I answered, "Name the date."

Phil and I did two cabaret concerts, two years in a row, at his house. The familiar feeling of transcending time and space settled in quickly during the first performance; it was a good-sized room, with about forty people seated in rows in front of us. The baby grand piano was perfectly tuned and resonant, and the acoustics were very good. Before I left for the concert, I sat on my bathroom floor with the hot water running in the shower, breathing in the steam, and wore a scarf to his house.

But I was in good voice. I didn't have to push or strain — all the notes, all the feelings, were there. Since I had lived in France and spoke the language fluently, the first half of our debut concert consisted of French cabaret songs. Phil accompanied me on the accordion for two of them (another of his hidden talents); all we were missing were wine glasses and smoldering cigarettes. Phil called my interpretation of Jacques Brel's *Ne Me Quitte Pas*, "a wrist-slitter."

The mood lifted with the second half of the program, which included cheerful songs by Rodgers & Hammerstein, Rodgers & Hart, and Stephen Sondheim. My encore was *Look to the Rainbow* by Burton Lane and Yip Harburg, one of my mother's favorites. I was sorry she wasn't there to hear it. In my mind, Uncle Larry was playing it and she was singing it along with me.

Because the room was relatively small and the audience close, I saw their faces reflect the emotions of each song, catching the irony, the humor, the happiness, the wistfulness, the loss, the despair. What a powerful medium the human voice is, I thought, that it can convey so many emotions so directly. The music and the lyrics were powerful. But the voice and the heart of the singer —who, in this moment, was happily, me — amplified the experience.

A brief time later, while I was continuing to take voice lessons and planning other concerts, I went in to have a lump on my thigh checked. I had been feeling fine, so I was shocked when I was diagnosed with Stage IV melanoma at Memorial Sloan Kettering.

Due to the treatments, which in the first two years ranged from immunotherapy to radiation and finally an extensive abdominal surgery, I didn't have the strength to sing. It was especially difficult to sing after surgery since it required cutting through the abdominal wall, and pushing aside the diaphragm and lungs. It took months for the abdominal muscles to knit back together. Even longer for me to sing without getting dizzy, or running the risk of herniating myself.

Six months later, the tumors grew back and I had to undergo a second abdominal surgery. When I was recovering, one of my oldest and dearest friends, Amy, invited me to join her for Friday night services at Central Synagogue, a reform temple near my house. I rolled my eyes in mock horror. I hadn't been to temple since the age of eight. The only reason my family occasionally went was because our temple, Rodeph Sholom, was just a few blocks from Barney Greengrass "the Sturgeon King" where my father loved to buy nova, sturgeon, sable, whitefish, three kinds of cream cheese, and a dozen bagels for the family's brunch.

Amy told me I should just go to enjoy the *music.* The Senior Rabbi, a former Cantor named Angela Buchdahl, is a beautiful young woman whose father is a Rumanian Jew and whose mother is a Korean Buddhist. Rabbi Angela accompanied herself on a guitar, interspersing folk songs with the traditional Sabbath music. I didn't want to hurt Amy's feelings, so the next Friday, I went to Shabbat services.

I was totally unprepared for the most thrilling musical experience I'd had in years. The singing continued almost uninterrupted for about an hour. Rabbi Angela and the Cantor were joined by four professional singers and five instrumentalists, who played both traditional and exotic instruments, adding richness and depth to the vocal lines.

These songs, a mix of ancient and modern, sounded and felt surprisingly familiar. I sang every one of them, following the transliterated texts as if I had been hearing and singing them my whole life. By the time we got to *Sh'ma Y'srael, Adonai Eloheinu, Adonai Echad*, one of the most beautiful, haunting melodies ever composed, I felt as if my voice were joining those of everyone in the Synagogue, as well as the eleven generations of Russian rabbis on my father's side of the family, and Jews all over the world who had ever lived and had sung this prayer.

My favorite song that evening, and every Shabbat since, consisted of one line from Psalm 126 of the Bible, *Those who sow in tears will reap in joy*. The simple line was set to music by a contemporary American composer, Debbie Friedman, and performed by vocalists, keyboard, guitar, bass, percussion, and a wailing clarinet.

At the end of the service, I couldn't move from my seat.

"So, what did you think?" asked Amy.

"It's a klezmer hootenanny. Nothing could make me happier. I will be here every Friday," I responded.

That week I joined the temple so I could sing those beautiful songs and have the transcendent experience of joining my voice to that of the rabbi, the cantor, the congregation, and the generations of Jews that had come before me. I still don't have my voice or my breath back completely, but at least I can be heard. Sometimes the people sitting in the seats in front of me turn around and ask, "Are you a professional singer? You have such a beautiful voice!"

Several weeks after my second abdominal surgery, I developed an obstruction and had to be hospitalized again, this time for fifteen days, and fed intravenously. About a week into my stay, Rabbi Angela came to visit. I was in a double room on the tenth floor of Memorial Sloan Kettering with a flimsy curtain separating my space from that of my roommate.

The rabbi and I sat and chatted for about an hour — about our children, her secretary who was about to retire, how much I liked her suede dress, how many times a week we could make it to the gym, how much we both loved Israeli date syrup, and our passionate love for singing.

"I usually say a prayer at the end of a hospital visit, but I get the feeling that you'd rather have a song," said the rabbi. I nodded enthusiastically.

"What would you like to sing?" she asked.

"The Debbie Friedman setting of Psalm 126," I answered without hesitation.

So, even though the day before I'd had a nasogastric tube down my throat, which I was afraid might damage my vocal cords (once a singer, always a singer), we launched into *Those who sow in tears, will reap in joy,* taking turns with melody and harmony.

Everything disappeared during that song: the hospital, the disease, mortality. What reappeared was the pure joy of singing, of connecting with another person through music. Once more I was incredibly grateful to be able to become one with sound. I couldn't tell where her voice began and mine ended. Adding to the beauty of the moment, our voices split into two vocal lines, in perfect harmony. Separate but joined.

As Rabbi Angela and I sang that simple sentence from an ancient psalm-turned-1960s folksong, I felt myself connecting with Sky Hollow Farm and Uncle Larry and Carnegie Hall and Madame Ryss and Beverly Sills and Phil and the other patient who shared my hospital room, and with the nurses and doctors in the hall who had stopped in front of our door just to listen.

September 2015

II

Growing Up

"If you don't recount your family history, it will be lost. Honor your own stories and tell them too. The tales may not seem very important, but they are what binds families and makes each of us who we are."

~ *Madeleine L'Engle*

I learned to read at an early age, thanks to my sister Jane.

The Price of Ear-Piercing

I WAS A REBELLIOUS teenager, who did what I was told *not* to, as often as possible.

My older sister, on the other hand, was an exemplary teenager. She didn't experiment with drugs or alcohol or sex and did everything that our parents expected of her. When she was away in the summer, she wrote long, detailed letters home. I wrote a weekly two-sentence postcard from camp, which was required for admission into the dining room for lunch every Sunday. These listed my accomplishments, most of which were exaggerated: "I completed the two-mile island swim." "I became a Junior Marksman." "I won the blue ribbon in the Good Hands class of the horse show."

My parents never remarked on these achievements so, after a while I stopped sending them. By mid-summer, I had achieved everything possible at camp anyway — or, at least, that's what I had reported.

In retrospect, I realize that my white lies were tests. I wanted to see if my parents were paying attention.

They weren't.

From the very start of her marriage, my mother worked for high profile volunteer organizations. And since she was smart, organized, efficient, and sincerely dedicated to whatever liberal cause that particular organization espoused, she always rose to the top. By the time I was in high school, she was president of the National Council of Women.

Her volunteer work consumed far more time than a paying job. She would put in a sixty- to eighty-hour week, which meant that I rarely saw her, and knew she had no idea what was going on in my, or my sister's, life.

When I was older and feeling charitable, I referred to my mother's style of child-rearing as benign neglect, not unlike Winifred Banks, Jane and Michael's suffragette mother in *Mary Poppins.* But as a teenager, there was no way I felt charitable about her priorities. Her own children ranked way below Third World children and the "poorest of the poor" in general. Her goal was to break the cycle of poverty, to provide them with opportunities for a better life. Highly commendable on the global scale, but not helpful in one-to-one parenting.

So I was pretty shocked when one of my little rebellious acts caused a huge reaction from her.

When I was fifteen, although my mother had forbidden me to pierce my ears, since she considered it "vulgar," I was dead-set on having it done. As I told her with impeccable teenage logic, "All my friends have had *their* ears pierced, and they shop for new earrings every Friday after school, which makes me feel very left out."

Thinking she'd never notice, one Friday afternoon after

school I went directly to Walker's Minerals, located on 61st and Lexington Avenue, a store which, as its name suggests, sold rocks and minerals and a few items of jewelry. It was where all my friends had had their ears pierced. It was not the most sanitary environment. Mr. Walker held an ice cube to the back of the ear lobe for a few seconds, then replaced the ice cube with a cork and hammered a gold stud through the lobe. His post-op directions were: "Leave them in for about ten days, twirl them, and put alcohol on them." I couldn't have been happier. Okay, so the hole on the left side was slightly lower than the right and both earlobes were flaming red, sore, and puffy. But I skipped home, feeling oh-so-grown-up, and oh-so-cool.

I'd returned home late, hoping to miss my parents, since I knew they were going out that evening, but mother was still there. Even though I had long hair, the glint of the gold earring must have caught her eye as I made a mad dash for my room.

"Come over here this minute!" she barked imperiously.

I steeled myself as I tried to walk nonchalantly into my parents' bedroom. She was seated in front of her dressing table, with its three hinged mirrored panels in a classic triptych over a mirrored table complete with mirrored drawers and sides.

"I forbade you to pierce your ears!" Her voice mounted in volume until she was yelling at the top of her lungs. "How *dare* you disobey me?"

She then took her right hand, balled it into a fist, and slammed it down onto the mirrored top. We both watched in fascination and horror as the glass shattered and a spiderweb of cracks spread out in all directions over the top of the dressing table. I glanced at the bottom of her hand, but there was no blood, so I decided I didn't have to feel guilty and shifted my focus to the floor.

I remained stock still and silent. I started to count backwards from twenty in French inside my head. The louder she yelled, the more able I was to make the sounds just bounce off my ears.

I was completely unresponsive, offering no explanation or apology. After she couldn't think of anything else to yell, and it was finally quiet, I spun on my heel and strode out of the room, slamming the door to my own room.

Post Script:

I was sure my mother had put a curse on my ears. Both ear lobes became very infected. They were so badly swollen and crusted that I couldn't rotate the earrings at all. It took weeks, applying Neosporin daily, to fight the infection. At several points I was tempted to remove the earrings and let the holes close and heal, but I didn't give in. I was going to ride out the curse.

Post Post Script:

When my own daughter was thirteen, she asked to have her ears pierced. I said "Great!" and made an appointment for her with a plastic surgeon, so it would be done properly, in an antiseptic environment. She had two symmetric piercings, which healed perfectly in a few days. I let her choose a few pairs of earrings at a renowned jeweler and we were both delighted.

Then, four years later, she came home late one afternoon with her hair in her face, which was odd, since she usually wore it in a ponytail. But after a minute, as she was trying to slink past me, she unconsciously tucked her hair behind one of her ears, and I noticed that she had had two more holes put in each ear: one at the top, which was secured with a square gold bolt, and another above the first hole on the lobe.

I looked at it for a second and said, "Oh, what luck! *Both* of your ears were falling off, but they were able to re-attach them to your head, and so attractively!"

She glared and rushed past me into her room, slamming the door behind her. Later, when I knocked on her door later to tell her that the chopped sirloin Florentine was ready, she came out and helped me set the table. Piercings forgotten, we chatted about our day. No yelling; no shattering of mirrors. All in all, I consider it progress.

June 1995

Bicentennial Birthday Party

ON JUNE 10, 1976, my mother sent out 100 invitations to America's 200th Birthday Party, to be celebrated on her terrace on July 4th. The terrace was key. Operation Sail 1976 would culminate with the Parade of Tall Ships on the Hudson. And by a stroke of luck, my mother's seventeenth-floor penthouse apartment, located on 78th Street at Riverside Drive, looked directly over the Hudson River Boat Basin. From her terrace, we'd have ringside seats to the Tall Ships Parade.

Despite her international philanthropic activities, first and foremost, Mother is a loyal and patriotic American. And what better way to celebrate America's birthday than to invite her closest friends to a viewing of the Tall Ships and a day-long barbecue on her seventeenth-floor penthouse.

The penthouse is not especially large, but the 5,000-square-foot terrace that wraps around it is huge. From the time my parents moved there in 1944, Mother — a gardener *manqué* — had planted everything from a Victory Garden to weeping willows. The terrace has been home to a pair of rabbits, Ike

& Mike; some Easter chicks, one of whom turned out to be a rooster; a pair of dachshunds, Antony & Cleopatra; and six puppies when Delilah, our first basset hound, gave birth there. Other key features included a gurgling fountain and a large outdoor grill with its own chimney.

When Mother mailed her invitations, we both assumed that most people would be away on a hot Sunday in July, and we'd end up with around fifty people. So we were shocked when the majority of our guests not only accepted, but most asked if they could bring family and friends. This brought the head count to around 200.

Mother was delighted.

We had ordered ice, an extra fridge, a free-standing freezer and four large ice tubs, as well as seven dozen chairs, twelve round tables with red and white checked tablecloths, and three industrial-size garbage cans. On July 1st, Mother and I met to organize the remaining tasks and start shopping.

On our way to the supermarket, we stopped in a diner and, over iced coffee, reviewed the legal pad filled with her lists. Here was her list for the supermarket:

- Two 15-lb. kosher salamis
- 150 kosher frankfurters and buns
- 40 lbs. of hamburger meat and buns
- 15 lbs. coleslaw
- 20 lbs. potato salad
- 9 dozen eggs for egg salad
- 6 bags of celery
- 10 lbs. mixed bean salad
- 2 watermelons

- 15 lbs. grapes
- Cheeses (wheels, wherever possible): Vermont Cheddar, Maytag Blue, Pepper Jack, Wisconsin Brie, Muenster
- 4 large green tins of Jacob's Biscuits for Cheese
- 5 dozen dill pickles (sour and half sour, no sweet)
- 4 squeeze bottles of Gulden's golden mustard
- 6 bottles of Heinz ketchup
- 3 jars of Hellman's mayo
- 4 dozen beefsteak tomatoes
- 8 heads of iceberg lettuce
- 2 dozen Vidalia sweet onions
- 4 large bags of M&Ms
- The Four P's (Stars of American junk food): pretzels, potato chips, peanuts, and popcorn
- 150 cans of soda
- 200 bottles of beer

When we left the diner, Mother spotted a display of huge red, white, and blue all-day suckers in the window of a candy store. The very definition of an impulse shopper, she immediately grabbed my arm and pulled me inside the store. "Give me as many of those as you've got!" she barked at the astonished young man behind the counter while pointing to the patriotic lollipops the size of salad plates. We exited the store with twenty-three huge red, white, and blue lollipops.

In addition to an open bar, manned by two students from Columbia University, Mother also planned on serving Abigail Adams' Authentic Punch in a giant crystal punch bowl. She had tasted this historic concoction at a reception for the PBS series,

Adams Chronicles, and, upon request, PBS had provided her with the recipe from Mrs. Adams' 18th century domestic diary. The ingredients included freshly-squeezed orange and lemon juices, strong tea, and a generous pour of rum topped off with a bottle of Champagne.

In a fit of patriotic fervor, Mother had ordered twenty-dozen Stars & Stripes-themed Good Humor popsicles. Max at the Good Humor depot was thrilled at the prospect of unloading such a large quantity of these occasion-specific novelty items to one customer, but I was leery. "Let's taste one before we confirm the order," I suggested. I found a Good Humor wagon a block from her house and bought one. It was truly vile. Bands of bright red, white, and blue ice. Colors and flavors not found in nature. I persuaded her to call Max and reduce that order to ten dozen, filling the rest with Toasted Almond, Strawberry Shortcake, Chocolate Éclair, and Chocolate Chip Candy. She called and left a message, then sent him a letter outlining the revised order and gave me a copy.

Freshly-baked cookies, delivered from our neighborhood bakery, rounded out the dessert list: four dozen chocolate chip, three dozen oatmeal, and three dozen snickerdoodles. But we'd have to pick up the fifteen fresh fruit pies — apple, cherry, and blueberry — from another store, downtown. We threw in a giant strawberry shortcake, to which Mother couldn't wait to add her own blueberries, reinforcing the patriotic theme.

For decorations, she'd purchased dozens of cardboard cylinders printed with a Revolutionary soldier design, like those British Christmas crackers. Instead of flowers, she planned to arrange these in straw baskets as table centerpieces. The terrace itself was already blooming with red, white, and blue petunias, pots of blue-violet pansies, and a riot of flaming red geraniums. On the walls, she planned to hang posters of Tall Ships, American flags, and maps. And for the foyer table: A replica of a full-rigged ship constructed from a mass of live cornflowers, daisies, and red carnations.

On the evening of July 2nd, Mother, Glen, my then-husband, David, and I met for dinner to divide the multitude of tasks ahead of us. Every time Mother assigned him an errand, I noticed David cringing slightly. So, it should not have come as a shock when, later that night, he announced to me that he had no intention of running around the city on a hot Saturday in July. Instead, he was catching the 7:15 a.m. train out to Westhampton to visit his friend Charlie, whose family had a house on the water.

I sank into a pool of anxiety, tossing and turning most of the night, reviewing lists in my head. When David's alarm went off at 6:30 a.m., he sprang out of bed, refreshed. His Ralph Lauren tote was packed with bathing trunks, sunglasses, *Bain de Soleil*, and a mystery novel. As he bent over to kiss me goodbye, I growled and buried my face in the pillow. I tried and failed to go back to sleep so, knowing that Mother was usually on her second cup of coffee by 6:30 a.m., I decided to give her a ring.

"What a beautiful day!" she exclaimed cheerily. "On terraces all up and down Riverside Drive, people are flying American flags." While having breakfast on the terrace, she'd seen U.S. battleships and even a few of the Tall Ships heading toward the 79th Street Boat Basin, visible directly below. Her enthusiasm helped to drop my anxiety level from chest pains to mere shortness of breath.

I casually mentioned that David had left for the beach, but unfazed, she said Glen would drive me to the wholesale pie bakery and the Good Humor outlet. "Be downstairs at ten," she directed.

I changed into a crisp white linen shirt, navy pants, high heeled white sandals, and big pearl earrings. As Grandma Isabel always said, *"you never know who you'll meet."*

When I climbed into Glen's blue Audi a few minutes after ten, I was clutching the envelope with Mother's scrawled directions. They didn't help. As we approached 23rd Street, I remembered that my stepfather's sense of direction was almost as bad as mine. At least he had an excuse, having lived in Connecticut most of his life.

We drove in ever-expanding circles, while I got to know a large cross-section of Village inhabitants by asking every third person for directions. Through luck and persistence, we finally found MacDougal Street but the addresses were in the hundreds, way above the number we were looking for. To compound our misery, MacDougal was a one-way street.

Aha. Bakery spotted. Instead of the large, highly professional operation I'd expected, this was a small corner store. I sprang from the car, leaving Glen with the motor running and paused before a large German Shepherd, asleep across the threshold of the open door. To enter, I would have to step over it. Inside, the store was empty except for a skinny older man with a nimbus of white hair framing his head.

"Pies for Mrs. Leet?" I called to him.

"Come on in, I've been expecting you," he responded.

He reached under the counter and started stacking grey cardboard pie boxes. I was about to step over the sleeping dog, when I noticed his eyes had opened and he was emitting a low growl. "Down, Schatzi", said the proprietor. Schatzi regarded me suspiciously.

It took two trips, but Glen and I managed to fit all the boxes in the trunk. I then asked the owner of the bake shop to direct us to 81 East Third Street, a distance of ten blocks complicated by crooked one-way streets with proprietary names.

As the bakery owner was launching into his explicit directions, his corpulent wife materialized, and assured me that her directions were better. Her husband, angry at being interrupted, increased the volume: "Make a left here and then go three blocks until you get to a church…" over his wife's shrill counterpoint: "Make a right, then go around the playground until you come to a dilapidated service station…" I hopped back into the car and told Glen to resume circling. Miraculously, we chanced upon Third Street in record time, but again, the numbers were too high.

"What's so funny?" I asked when I heard Glen chuckling to himself.

"I told your mother this morning," he said, "considering our sense of direction, Aileen and I may just disappear into the heart of the Village and never be heard from again."

Ten minutes later, we arrived at the Good Humor headquarters. When I counted eighteen motorcycles parked diagonally in front of the correct address, I thought there'd been some mistake. But, as it turned out, Good Humor shared the building with the Hell's Angels. Casually draped over a few of the bikes, the sidewalk, and the steps, were several of the Angels themselves, resplendent in black leather vests, greasy pony tails, mirrored sunglasses, bandana headbands, and tattoos.

I took a deep breath, flung open the car door, and strode purposefully up the stoop looking, I hoped, like a person on a mission. I thought seriously about "whistling a happy tune" but then thought that was hitting the wrong tone. Inside, hundreds of men were milling about, screaming at each other in different languages, none dressed in the kid-friendly Good Humor man uniform and cap. The floor was littered with shredded cardboard and, in one corner, sparks shot into the air as an electric buzz saw ran through huge blocks of smoke-fogged dry ice.

I drew myself up to my full five-foot-three-inches and shouted, "I gotta see the manager!" Ignored, I repeated myself, even louder. Two burly young men in ripped undershirts moved, toward me, making obscene kissing noises and rolling their eyes suggestively. I positioned myself behind one of the wagons when Max the manager brushed them aside and walked up to me.

"Yeah, waddya want?" he said. I thrust a carbon copy of Mother's most recent communiqué into his hand. It confirmed the order for twenty dozen Good Humors. I held onto the check, in a separate envelope, explaining that he'd get it once I confirmed the assortment included the mix of flavors, "not just Stars and Stripes," I insisted.

"The red, white, and blue would be the hit of your party," Max pressed.

No way was I leaving without Toasted Almond, Strawberry

Shortcake, Chocolate Éclair, and Chocolate Chip Candy. "If it's so popular," I retorted, "You'll have no trouble unloading them on other patriotic customers!"

"You drive a hard bargain, lady." He sighed and shrugged his shoulders before disappearing for an unconscionably long time. Just as I was tempted to step outside and offer two Hell's Angels twenty bucks to accompany me back inside, he reappeared with the boxes on a dolly.

He had packed them in a large carton, resembling a small coffin, with wisps of smoke from the dry ice seeping out of the corners, and ordered someone to get a dolly and take them out to my car. On the stoop, a few of the Hells Angels stopped passing a joint long enough to politely ask if they could come to the party. "Maybe next time," I replied cheerily, "we've run out of room. But happy Fourth to all of you!"

One of the Angels offered me a hit off his joint, which was tempting, but all I really wanted to do was get uptown as fast as city traffic lights would permit. "Floor it!" I said to Glen, who rarely drove over twelve miles an hour.

When we pulled up in front of the building, the doorman was mystified by the coffin in the back of the car, emitting wisps of smoke. "Nothing to be alarmed about. Just need to get the popsicles upstairs quickly," I said.

I glanced at my watch, and was horrified. Not by the time, but by my inability to tell it. That morning, I had accidentally put on my minimalist Movado museum-piece watch. With its round black face, the watch features a single gold dot where the twelve should be. "What time is it, Mother?" I asked, as we loaded the popsicles into her rented freezer.

"Two o'clock!" she said brightly.

I have trouble telling time on a watch with twelve clear Arabic numerals, so it was an act of sadism on my husband's part to buy me a watch with one gold dot. "Got to run — I was supposed to be at Karen's at one," I said, banging on the elevator button. By now, according to my schedule, I should have boiled 108 eggs.

Karen Lee, a professional Chinese cook, caterer, and teacher, as well as an unbelievably good friend had volunteered to help with the party prep. Indeed, I entered her kitchen to find two huge aluminum bowls on the counter, heaped high with steaming eggs. Since they were too hot to handle, I decided to watch her prepare her delicious spicy eggplant dish for the party. Karen triangle-cut red and green peppers with speed and dexterity. It was like having my very own PBS special. I was settling in to watch her smash garlic cloves with the flat side of her cleaver when I realized that the eggs were not going to peel themselves.

Ideally, one gentle tap should allow the shell of a hard-boiled egg to slide off in large smooth pieces. Since life can be cruel, however, I soon found myself smashing all sides of the eggs. The jagged shells left shallow cuts all over my fingers and bits of egg white often came off with the shell. Karen took pity on me and began to pitch in. We filled the bowls with ice water and, about an hour later, when all the eggs were peeled with a reasonable ratio of white to yolk, Karen returned to stir-frying the eggplant.

Time to chop the 108 eggs. I could only chop about six at a time, so the entire batch took an hour. Once all the eggs were chopped, I added a vat of Hellman's, some Dijon, lots of salt and pepper, and some fresh dill in small batches. By the time I was finished, I never wanted to see, peel, or eat another egg before the Tricentennial.

Karen and I lugged the huge containers of eggplant appetizer and egg salad over to the penthouse. Mother was marching around the apartment with two pens stabbed into her chignon, with her eyeglasses around her neck on a chain, clutching her lists while making split-second decisions. Karen left immediately.

I picked up a Post-it pad and, armed with a red Magic Marker, followed closely on her heels as she zoomed from house to terrace and back. "Pies! Pickles! Hot Dogs!" she proclaimed, pointing to strategic positions while I scurried behind her scribbling on Post-its and smacking them down in the corresponding spots. We then began putting out non-perishables: paper goods, beverages, and those indispensable "P" foods. Mother then decided it was time to sample an item beginning with M, namely a Martini, and went to find a suitable pitcher, stemmed glasses, Bombay Sapphire Gin, vermouth, ice, and olives. We made up a batch.

"Happy Birthday, America!" she said, and we clinked glasses.

"I've survived a growling German Shepherd, pot-smoking Hell's Angels, lascivious Good Humor men, and the stab of over 100 eggshell shards," I sighed, taking a large sip of martini. "You're lucky I made it back in one piece."

I held out my right hand in a subtle bid for sympathy. It looked like I had tried to put a feral cat into a cage.

She ignored my hand.

"What a great story!" she exclaimed and took another sip. "You'll have to tell it tomorrow at the party."

July, 1976

Attack of the Giant Moth

ONE SUMMER NIGHT WHEN Ariel was about twelve, we were watching a movie in my room with Ollie the English Spaniel curled up between us. About halfway through, she happened to glance up at the painting above my bed.

"Hey, mom, when did you get this new painting?"

"What new painting?" I said, only paying partial attention since I was engrossed in the movie.

"The one with the brown mosaic butterfly. I liked the line drawing more."

I froze. Very slowly, I tilted my head up and around, and she was right: centered perfectly on top of the framed Philip Grausman line drawing of a female nude above my bed, there was a brown moth with blue spots and the wingspan of a condor.

She and I both let out ear-piercing screams, leaped off the bed and ran out of the room as fast as we could, leaving our half-asleep spaniel on the bed. We slammed the door so hard, it shook in its frame. Clutching each other and gasping for breath, we ran across the hall into her room, slamming that door as well.

"What is that creature?" she asked when she had enough breath to talk.

"It's not a butterfly, but I didn't think moths came in giant sizes," I responded.

"Well, whatever it is, I'm sleeping in here tonight."

"And you think I'd set foot back in that Chamber of Horrors with a gargantuan flying beast hovering above my head? Just lucky you have two beds in your room!"

We heard a scratching on my bedroom door.

"Oh my God," said Ariel, blanching, "the moth is trying to get out."

"Unless it is a really scary mutant, darling, I don't think the moth could make scratching noises," I responded, trying to sound calm and reasonable. "I think it's Ollie. We must have scared him to death with all our shrieking. And anyway, it's time for his walk."

We looked at each other, knowing that one of us would have to open the door to let the dog out.

"If I promise you a shopping spree at the store of your choice," I said, trying desperately to come up with a tempting bribe, "will you not only open the door to let Ollie out, but also open the window so the Killer Moth can flap back out to another perch?"

There was a protracted silence.

"Okay," she finally agreed reluctantly, "*Any* store of my choice, including Barney's, and only if you promise not to try to influence my choices by muttering negative comments under your breath in the fitting room. "

"Deal! And don't worry — I'll be right behind you in the hallway," I said, knowing those were words of little comfort.

I felt guilty and awful. I was passing on an irrational fear of insects to my daughter. What a terrible role model. But after a minute, she steeled herself, walked slowly across the hall and gingerly opened the door, letting the anxious dog out.

"It's still there," she whispered. "Now I have to walk to the other side of the bed to open the window. It's going to hear me and fly off the painting into my hair."

"Excuse me? You think a moth has such good hearing? It didn't budge when the two of us were screaming like banshees! Moths are deaf. And they have almost no vision, either," I said, authoritatively, making this up as I went along.

She dashed across the room, shoved the closest window open, galloped back out and slammed the door again. All on one breath.

I gave her a huge hug and congratulated her on her bravery. I said that acts of tremendous courage use a lot of adrenalin, which burns a lot of calories, thereby justifying a large bowl of chocolate mint chip ice cream. She agreed.

After our celebratory snack, we went to sleep in her room, wondering how the movie ended.

The next morning, now feeling guilty about having made my daughter go back into my bedroom, I crept in there myself, before she woke up.

There was Grausman's elegant drawing, in all of its simple splendor. The outline of a nude, no moth in sight.

Later, since we thought people might be skeptical of our claim, we looked up giant moth and this is what we found:

Antheraea polyphemus, the Polyphemus moth, is a North American member of the family *Saturniidae*, the giant silk moth. It is a tan-colored moth, with a large wingspan. The most notable feature of the moth is its large, purplish eyespots on its two hindwings. The eyespots give it its name – from the Greek myth of the cyclops Polyphemus. It is widespread in continental North America. The caterpillar can eat 86,000 times its weight at emergence in a little less than two months.

~*Wikipedia*

Since Ariel and I were both fans of Greek mythology, I then looked up Polyphemus, to discover he was the giant son of Poseidon and Toosa. He was the most famous of the Cyclops, described by Homer in *The Odyssey*. He was first known as a "savage man-eating giant."

Yup. That sounded about right.

August 1990

Postscript: The report of this event was a collaboration between Aileen and Ariel. Her memory of the event was better than mine.

January 2019

Nice Bacon and Eggs

"When you wake up in the morning, Pooh," said Piglet
at last, "what's the first thing you say to yourself?"
"What's for breakfast?" said Pooh.
"What do you say, Piglet?"
"I say, I wonder what's going to happen
exciting *today?*" said Piglet.
Pooh nodded thoughtfully, "It's the same thing," he said.

A. A. Milne

WHEN MY SISTER AND I were small, my mother used to say good night to us in a particular way. Instead of "Good night, sleep tight" or "pleasant dreams," she would say, "Good night, nice bacon and eggs." I thought this was what everybody's mother said, so when my daughter Ariel was growing up, I naturally said the same thing after I'd tucked her in and kissed her good night.

When Ariel was around ten and started going to sleepovers, she noticed that nobody else's mother said "Nice bacon and eggs" when they tucked their children into bed. "Where in the world did that expression come from?" she asked accusingly one evening, while we were having dinner with my mother.

"From my mother," I replied and since my mother was just across the table, I immediately turned to confront her.

"Where on earth did *you* get that dumb expression?" I asked.

"I made it up," she said, cheerfully. "Breakfast is a meal I always look forward to — the best reason to get up in the morning — and my favorite breakfast is bacon and eggs, so I thought it would be a nice last thought, before going to sleep."

I thought that Ariel would ask me to delete it from my vocabulary and go back to the traditional pre-sleep wishes that she heard at her friends' houses. But by then, my daughter and I had been saying it for so long that we couldn't stop.

Several years later, when her daughter was born, I overheard her tucking her daughter in. "Nice bacon and eggs," she cooed.

I found myself smiling broadly, realizing that there were now three generations that were using that silly expression. It had become a Robbins tradition.

Mother was right. Cholesterol be damned, my favorite breakfast is still bacon and eggs, and it's still the best reason to get up in the morning.

November 2018

Running Down Stairs

...and Other Life Lessons I Learned at Brearley

I'M PRETTY QUALIFIED TO reflect on my Brearley experience, since I went here for *twenty-six years*. Let me explain: First thirteen years, I attended; second thirteen years, my daughter attended. The second round gave me a different perspective and was infinitely more enjoyable. I didn't have to take exams, but I still got to sing Christmas carols in the front hall.

In some ways, the school has changed a lot in fifty years, but in other fundamental ways, it is very much the same. Yes, there is much greater diversity in the student body; the science and math departments are stronger; there are many more athletic options and playing fields, and I sure wish I'd had the option to take Mandarin. But the core values remain the same, and I believe, more than ever, that Brearley graduates are the best and brightest. Okay, so we're accused of being overachievers; but there's nothing wrong with living a productive life, burning with intellectual curiosity, and wanting to give back.

So what was it in my years at Brearley that contributed to a productive life? Let me share my little ten-point list with you.

1. How to Write and Edit

The best lesson I learned at Brearley was how to organize thoughts and substantiate an argument, with an introduction, an outlined exposition (which my daughter calls "the body") and a conclusion. I still have undying respect for an effective topic sentence, which should lead out of the paragraph before, and into the paragraph that follows. My writing skills helped me to get articles published and to be hired for challenging jobs. These skills also contributed to major careers of my classmates; the most dramatic example is Lydia Davis, who won the Man Booker International Prize in 2013, while others have published short stories, novels, and articles, as well as academic tracts and legal briefs.

2. How to Take Great Notes

Coming from an all girls' school and having no brothers, I had no idea how to deal with boys once I got to a co-ed college. The only way I could initially relate to them was by giving them my outlined and typed notes from class. It gave me the illusion that I was really popular, especially with members of the Stanford football team, although I got wise to it by my second semester. I still obsessively take notes at meetings and conferences and I find my colleagues often ask me for them. For better or worse, it has led me to be invited to sit on a number of boards and take minutes.

3. How to Recognize, Appreciate, and Seek Brilliance

The high level of academic excellence which I experienced

at Brearley unfortunately was never reached at any other of my educational institutions, even though I went through B.A., M.A. and Ph.D. programs at very good schools. The person who set the gold standard for me was Ruth Carpenter. She fostered a love of literature that is central to my enjoyment of living and I am always looking for exciting new books to read and plays to attend. I thought my memory was greater than the reality, but when I attended Parents' Day for my daughter, thirty years after I had Mrs. Carpenter for English, I sat in on her Shakespeare class and was transfixed. She was more interesting, more challenging, and more inspiring than I even remembered. My daughter and I are constantly looking for other Mrs. Carpenters, as I'm sure many of you are, as well.

4. How to Run Down Stairs

My main athletic achievement at this school was running up, and especially down, a flight of stairs in about eleven seconds. I wasn't much of a star in any organized sport — never really saw the point of basketball, softball, or hockey; felt vaguely simian on the rings, and always wanted to run for cover during dodge ball. It was a huge relief when many of us found we developed crippling cramps and could be excused from gym. I often still take subway steps two at a time.

5. How to be Silent

Having had to observe the rule of no talking in the elevator for twenty-six years, to this day, I am stone quiet in elevators. Or at least for twelve floors. After that, I breathe a sigh of relief and immediately engage in a lively conversation with anyone along for the ride, which frequently includes complete strangers.

6. How to Appreciate the Arts

It was a true thrill when my art works were chosen for the Kunz collection; I felt a surge of pride every time I caught sight of my pastel still-life adorning the front hall. In fact, it was so inspiring that I signed up for a life drawing course at the Art Students League when I was a junior. I must admit, however, that I was totally shocked when I walked into my first class and saw a nude male model posing on a stool. It took all of my resolve not to turn and flee. Somehow, I managed to get through the two-hour class and the three-month course and developed a huge respect and love for drawing and painting of all kinds.

7. How to Strive for Perfection

Although it was by no means the rule in my academic life at Brearley, I was always thrilled to see the occasional Very Good handwritten on the upper right-hand corner of a quiz, exam, or paper. (The alumna office recently informed me that they have done away with word grades, and now use plain old letter grades.) The problem didn't arise until I entered the work force and was truly disappointed when I no longer saw even a simple VG on the top of an article sent to an editor, or a speech written for a client.

8. How to burn with Intellectual Curiosity

I am endlessly, some might say, pathologically curious. I read constantly, take courses, go to lectures, watch PBS, listen to NPR, and am in a career where I get to interview interesting people. But sometimes I think it is a curse as well as a blessing, since I always feel I should be taking up a new musical instrument or learning a new language, especially one with an unfamiliar alphabet. Having nothing to read during a quiet time drives me to distraction and contributes to my having memorized the backs and sides of many cereal boxes.

9. How to make and keep life-long, unconditionally loving friendships

This is as true for my daughter as for me, so I think it is fair to take the anecdotal as universal. My best friends in the world today are former classmates. Even though we now live in different cities, we speak or write constantly and visit each other multiple times a year. Not only was a Brearley classmate my daughter's maid of honor, but she texts around three Brearley girls every week.

10. How to Appreciate The Brearley Sisterhood

The Yaya Sisterhood pales in comparison to the Brearley Sisterhood. Ours is far-reaching, since it applies not only to close friends within one's own class or a sibling's class, but also to perfect strangers. When we discover they attended the school, there is an immediate and meaningful connection. At a fund-raiser for an opera company last summer, I randomly sat next to a young woman, and within a few minutes discovered that she had gone to Brearley. We plunged into an animated, rapid-fire conversation, barely stopping to breathe, and probably would have talked all night had there not been a performance to attend. We had so much in common, I felt as if I were reconnecting with an old friend. Sharing the Brearley experience for many years — for me, childhood and adolescence — is like sharing parents; there are many formative forces at play which shape who you are and how you see and deal with the world.

Thank you for giving me this opportunity to reflect back on fifty years, and to see how The Brearley School has shaped my life. Yes, it gave me a superb academic education, but it also offered much more: It instilled values, and gave me lifelong friendships, as well as satisfaction from professional achievements; it has helped me live my life with meaning. You must admit, it's a little daunting to read the Brearley Bulletin and to see the achievements of your classmates, but I bet you don't just read about your own class; you continue to read, with awe, the notes of the classes that came before and after. I've accomplished a few things in the past five decades, but even though it feels like half of what many others have, I am exceptionally proud to be part of a school whose graduates contribute so much to the lives of others.

Speech delivered by Aileen at her 50th Reunion at The Brearley School
May 2, 2015

III

Generations

Four generations: I'm on the left next to Grandma Isabel Elowski who is holding my daughter, Ariel Kate Friedman (now Ariel Fantasia) on her lap. Mildred Robbins Leet, who Ariel calls Gaggy, sits next to them. My sister, Jane Maria Robbins, is seated in front.

We're Off to See the Princess

IN MAY OF 1989, Ariel and I went to London for four days, right in the middle of the school year, because my mother was one of three honorees receiving Women of the World Awards from the British organization, WomenAid. Millie was in good company. The other two women were Professor Wangari Maathai, Founder of the Green Belt Movement in Kenya, and Mother Teresa, Founder, Missionaries of Charity.

In 1979, my mother had co-founded The Trickle Up Program, a microenterprise nonprofit organization that sought to break the cycle of poverty. The award would be presented by Her Royal Highness the Princess of Wales, Diana, whom we would meet personally at a private reception before the Awards Luncheon at Grosvenor House in Park Lane. My mother would be seated on the dias, next to Princess Di.

When my mother was notified of the award, several weeks in advance, we were all thrilled for her; but I wasn't going to yank Ariel out of Brearley to go to London for the ceremony. Then I thought to myself, *when is Ariel ever going to get to shake hands and curtsey to Lady Di?* So, what the hell, I decided we had to be there and booked our flights.

During the overnight flight on Friday, we took a few fitful catnaps before the plane touched down around 7:00 a.m. An hour later, we arrived at The Royal Horse Guards, right across from Buckingham Palace and, although the hotel's location was swell, the rooms were basically stalls. When Ariel and I stretched out on our double bed, we could touch the walls on either side. Aside from a miniscule television at the foot of the bed which we could touch with our toes, the room's only other object was a pants presser, stuck into the wall. The place was so grim that by Sunday, we were thrilled to move to The Berkshire on Oxford Street.

After a two-hour nap, my best friend Naomi Sorkin, a ballerina who had been living in London for the past six years, appeared on our doorstep and the three of us hit the streets. I had decided, after ransacking my full-to-overflowing closet in New York, trying everything on three times, and finally packing a few boring choices, that I had absolutely *nothing* to wear, so I had to go shopping in London. We grabbed a bite of lunch and ran over to Brown's, which has several haute couture boutiques under one roof.

Over the course of the next three hours, I tried on dozens of suits, skirts, blouses, scarves, and jackets. With input from Naomi, Ariel, two salesgirls, and the owner of the store, who were all impressed by the reason for the purchase, I finally decided on a stunning and simple little ensemble from Sonia Rykiel. I had been instructed to wear something "elegant but not glitzy" and the restrained green suit — somewhere between forest and emerald with black trim — fit the bill.

The new outfit screamed out for some accessories, so I also bought a pair of black stockings, a new pair of high black heels, and a silk scarf. Not that I needed another item of clothing or accessory, but if you can't justify buying a new outfit when you're meeting the Princess of Wales, when can you?

By then Ariel was falling off her stool with exhaustion and I was feeling guilty for having taken up so much of her time shopping for me, so we swung round to the flagship Laura Ashley store to perk her up. After choosing a few sweaters and skirts, we did the only civilized thing, namely screech off to Claridge's for High Tea. The display was staggering: Skinny little tea sandwiches, made with butter, not mayonnaise, of course, which were followed by hot scones served with Devon clotted cream and thick strawberry jam, further followed by pastries: Lemon curd tartlets, mini eclairs, mini madeleines and chocolate shortbread. By this time, our eyes were glazed and nobody could breathe. I was beginning to worry seriously about the size six Sonia with the straight skirt.

But never mind, I rationalized. We would just skip dinner.

When we returned to our hotel I received a phone call from my friend Neil, an American who was in London on business. Would we join him for dinner?

"Well, we'd love to see you," I told Neil, "but we've just eaten for twelve, so we'll have drinks with you and then go home."

"Great! See you at 8:00," said Neil.

We met Neil and his friends for drinks at The Draycott, one of the most beautiful hotels I'd ever seen in my life. After a few rounds of drinks, we all trooped off to dinner at a little Italian restaurant in the neighborhood.

Famous last words: "I'll just pick."

Four courses later, Ariel and I stumbled back to our stall — I mean *hotel room* — where my mother and Glen were anxiously waiting up for us. They had taken the morning flight, and had not arrived until 10:30 p.m. By now it was midnight and she assumed we had been carried off by gypsies. Leaping over a corner of the mattress, I opened the six-inch-wide closet and whipped out my new green outfit for the luncheon. To my horror, mother took one look, frowned, and said, "Don't you think that's a little flashy, dear?"

What else had I packed? she wanted to know, and I disconsolately pried the olive drab suit from the closet. The long skirt, which came down to my ankles, was topped with a black herringbone tweed jacket and finished with an olive silk shirt. It was dull and conservative. Mother thought it was perfect.

Sunday, we visited more friends and went to lunch with Ann Tweedy, one of my oldest and best friends from Brearley, whose her main residence was Harthill Castle in Aberdeenshire, Scotland, but who also had a flat in London and would be attending the awards luncheon. Then we swooped by Naomi's beautiful flat, which looks out over an enormous rose garden. We left to have dinner with the Freemans — friends from New York who had just moved to London, and whose oldest daughter was one of Ariel's best friends. They took us to a restaurant called

Sticky Fingers which is owned by one of the Rolling Stones and is a Hard Rock Café rip-off, except they only play Rolling Stones songs. At top volume, of course. Sticky Fingers does not make the list of restaurants in the great cities of the world to which I would most like to return.

Monday was another exceptionally beautiful day; unlike any weather I had experienced in London. Ariel had been looking forward to the famous London pea-soup fog, so she was a little disappointed when it was bright and sunny. We left in plenty of time for the awards luncheon, arriving at The Grosvenor House by noon, since guests must always arrive well in advance of royalty. The Princess was expected at 12:30, and she arrived right on schedule.

The honorees and their families or friends were escorted into a private reception room and we all did get to meet her personally, each and every one of us. H.R.H. the Princess of Wales wore a gorgeous dove grey suit which skimmed the knee with a shell-pink satin blouse. She looked smashing. Tall and willowy, with beautiful skin and, as Ariel and I agreed, the most amazing cornflower blue eyes we'd ever seen. She was engaging, in a formal but seemingly accessible way, looking directly in the eyes of every one of the guests as she spoke a sentence or two. Even though my knees were knocking when I was introduced to her, I did manage to creak out a curtsey and mumble "Your Royal Highness," as did Ariel. We had been practicing curtseys for hours.

The luncheon was a success and a new food experience for Ariel; she was fascinated by the vegetable terrine, glued together with aspic, and cut vertically, so the string beans looked like little green circles, which was followed by another *trompe l'oeil* dish, *saumon en croûte.* Mother gave a wonderful speech and they showed a short film of her working in the field in Bangladesh with Trickle Up grant winners. The Princess then presented each WomenAid recipient with a large crystal, hand-carved globe on a mahogany base with a little gold-faced clock.

"Just think how many Trickle Up businesses we could have started with the money they spent on this!" Mother whispered to me after the luncheon.

But underneath, I think she was pleased with the recognition, not for herself, but for the organization she had worked so hard to build.

Millie, left, receiving the crystal globe
from H.R.H. Princess Di

First Person Plural

ON WEDNESDAY, JUNE 20, 1990, five days before my eleven-year-old daughter Ariel was to leave for summer camp for two months, I made an appointment with her pediatrician, Dr. Seed. I'd noticed a small white bump on her clavicle, almost like an insect bite, that hadn't changed size, shape or color in a week and, without alarming Ariel, I wanted him to take a look.

Ariel would be coming directly from her three-hour tennis clinic to meet me there. Although Dr. Seed was a brilliant pediatrician, his restraint sometimes drove me nuts. Ariel had been his patient since birth but he had showed no emotion — in his eyes, his face, or his voice — over the past eleven years.

For once, his office was not crowded, so the exam began a few minutes after she arrived, still in her tennis whites. Watching him examine her I thought, *Well, there's a healthy specimen* — tan, slender, muscular, with thick, honey-colored hair that could barely be contained in any type of hairclip. She looked bored and was mad that I had dragged her to the doctor; she was hungry, and wanted to go to J.G. Melon with some friends for a hamburger.

Dr. Seed ran his fingers around her jaw line and then palpated the lump on her collarbone. He muttered to himself more than to us, "Hmm. An enlarged lymph node." I had no idea whether that was significant, or in what way, but I did notice his reaction. He actually turned white — the blood drained out of his face — and he cleared his throat several times. When he spoke, his voice actually sounded shaky.

"She needs a complete blood work-up and a set of chest x-rays. I will call ahead to Dr. Callahan, the radiologist, and he will see you immediately; take a cab to 420 East 72nd Street."

I tried not to react to his tone, no less his words.

"Come on, darling," I said to Ariel, "let's just run by for x-rays, then I'll take you to Melon's for lunch."

We arrived at the radiologist's office in a few minutes. My anxiety was steadily rising; obviously, Dr. Seed had called ahead and told the nurse to have someone see her as soon as she arrived, even though there were lots of people ahead of us in the waiting room.

They wouldn't let me accompany her while the technician took the x-ray, so I paced up and down a long, ugly white hallway and waited for a doctor to appear. Several minutes later, I spotted one of the doctors and grabbed hold of his forearm. "Can you give me any idea what the x-rays have shown?" I asked, not even identifying whose x-rays, but he knew.

He placed his hands on my shoulders and looked straight in my eyes.

"Don't worry; whatever it is, they have a cure."

"A cure for *what*?" I asked.

"I'm sorry; I can't tell you anything else. I will speak to her pediatrician, and he'll call you as soon as you get home."

Ariel got dressed quickly and didn't even ask about lunch. Neither of us were hungry.

When we first walked into our apartment, it seemed like a haven. Everything was just as we left it, when life was still normal. Ollie the spaniel was barking his head off, I tripped over a bag from the cleaners, and the *New York Times* was splayed all over the dining room table. Ariel scooped up the dog and ran into my room, where she and the dog landed in the middle of my queen-size bed. I was beginning to breathe a little more easily when the phone rang.

It was Dr. Seed.

He didn't give me any preparation — no "Are you sitting down?" or "Perhaps you would like to come to my office, so I can tell you in person…" No. He just blurted out, "It's probably lymphoma, but if she's lucky it's Hodgkin's."

I looked up and saw my daughter in her white tennis shorts, sitting two feet away from me, cross-legged on my bed, wrestling the dog. I felt as if a safe had fallen on me and my entire body had been compressed to approximately one-half an inch. Underground. I felt a funny tingly sensation on the top of my scalp, along with a slight ringing in my ears.

I also realized I could display no reaction to Dr. Seed's last sentence and gave myself a mental slap. I had to appear normal and in control, so I didn't frighten my daughter. A second later, clutching the phone very hard, I answered Dr. Seed.

"Yes, Dr. Seed, I understand. Just tell me where we should go now."

"I've called ahead to the Pediatric Oncology Department of New York Hospital on 68th and York. Dr. Patricia Giardina is waiting for you."

"Got it. Dr. Giardina," I repeated, scribbling it down on the back of an envelope near the phone. "OK, we'll be there in about ten minutes."

I hung up the phone and glanced at Ariel, who was looking apprehensive.

"Mommy, what did Dr. Seed say?" she asked.

"He said we had to go to New York Hospital for a few more tests, honey, so just throw some clothes in a bag. Don't worry; I'll pack a bag, too, since they'll let me stay if you have to stay."

"How long will I have to stay?"

"Oh, not long; just a day or two," I answered, not having the slightest idea whether it would be two days or twenty. "But don't worry; whatever it is, they can take care of it."

"What is *it*?" she asked.

"Well, they don't know yet, which is why you have to have some more tests, but they'll know by tomorrow. Come on honey, let's get going — the sooner we get there, the sooner we can come home. Dr. Seed told me to ask for Dr. Giardina; she's a very nice doctor, who specializes in kids your age."

I did not say that Dr. Giardina specializes in pediatric oncology.

By Thursday afternoon, most of the tests had been completed: Biopsy of the lymph node that had popped out on her shoulder blade, CT Scan, MRI, gallium scan, endless blood tests. Dr. Giardina came in to the clinic to discuss Ariel's diagnosis and prognosis. She was calm, clear, reassuring, and gentle; you could tell she loved every one of the children in this clinic, and would do everything in her power to heal them.

The diagnosis was Stage IV Hodgkin's Disease, which presented itself as a mediastinal mass — a huge, malignant tumor — which took up almost half of Ariel's thoracic cavity. Because it lay between the heart and lungs, it was totally inoperable but could be eradicated with a fairly radical, long-range protocol: Two years of chemotherapy and radiation.

Nine years later, at a writing seminar in Italy, I was finally able to write about this two-year period in Ariel's and my life, a period which I could barely talk about, no less write about during those nine years. But once I started writing — for a very supportive, loving group of other writers, all women — I couldn't stop. On the first night, I wrote twenty-two pages without a break and then only stopped because dinner was served. The following morning, at the insistence of the teacher, Phyllis Theroux, I read it aloud to the class.

The first thing which struck me was that I was able to put words on paper and then read them aloud without breaking down. But my second observation was equally interesting: I realized how often in this unedited text I had used "we" instead of "she" when describing my daughter's illness, therapy, and recovery.

I realized that there had been a blurring of boundaries, both then as well as now, as I was remembering and writing about that time. It was as if I had put her back inside me, so I could protect her. I didn't realize how unhealthy this closeness could be, but my daughter did, and after the initial shock had passed, she found ways to protect herself.

Since she was only eleven at the time, and since I was the main caretaker (her father fainted at the sight of a needle), I accompanied her on every single trip to the hospital, for every test, every procedure. These ranged from height, weight, and blood pressure to EKGs to see if the adriamycin had damaged the muscle of the heart, to the injection of radioactive gallium for a special scan (this was also intriguing, since we watched as the doctor removed the liquid from a six-inch lead casing before injecting it into her vein).

During this time, there were physical connections as well as emotional ones — I always squeezed her hand as they searched for a vein, to take blood for the bi-weekly tests, or to set up an IV. During this time, we would lock eyes, and I would quiz her on multiplication tables, distracting her from the endless, and often futile, needle sticks.

When she had to stay overnight in the hospital, I would sit next to her bed on a reclining chair which I quickly named "Snap, the Magic Clam" because of its propensity to snap back to an upright position if I shifted my weight one inch forward, backward, or sideways. I would chat endlessly with her whenever she couldn't sleep and would leave my hand near the pillow.

There were other types of physical connections and heightened awarenesses that evolved between us. By the second chemo cycle, I reached the point where I could tell her temperature by putting my hand almost anywhere on her body. This was crucial, because several of the drugs caused her to run a fever, and although anything up to 101° was acceptable, if the temperature rose above 102°, she had to be hospitalized and an antibiotic IV had to be set up. I could tell, from a touch, the difference between 101° and 102°, so we did not have to go through the agony of sitting with a thermometer in her mouth for three minutes.

The physical closeness brought back quite a wonderful memory. It reminded me of breast-feeding my daughter. I remembered being amazed and filled with awe when I brought her home from the hospital and realized, the first night, that two things were happening simultaneously: I was waking up, not only because my breasts were beginning to hurt as they filled up with milk, but also because I could hear her beginning to cry because she was hungry.

But here it was, eleven years later, and I was very aware that Ariel was not one month or one year old; she was an adolescent, entering the crucial stage of separation. So I realized that, as reassuring as it was to have her mother by her side — someone who loved her unconditionally — it also impeded normal emotional growth. It was not that she was regressing; it was just that she did not have the luxury of rejecting me to move forward toward independence.

Soon enough, however, there were glimpses. The first one came during the second cycle, when the four different chemo drugs, given in the same sequence, became "known devils". We knew her reaction to each of them: How severe it would be, how long it would last. One night, after several hours of vomiting, as I waited in the room, sitting on her bed, Ariel returned from the bathroom and said to me, "Stop hovering! I hate it when you hover!" It struck us both as funny, and I beat a hasty retreat (although remaining within earshot).

The most dramatic example of her healthy instincts of separation came at the end of her treatment. She had finished the six cycles of chemotherapy and was on her last day of radiation. When we returned home from the hospital that afternoon, she raced into her room and began to dismantle the second twin bed, in which I had spent many vigilant nights. In less than an hour, with the help of the super, it had been moved to the storage room in the basement. I never spent another night in her room again.

During the next five years, until she left for college, her separateness was as intense as our closeness had been. I was not just peripheral or unnecessary; it was as if I were viewed as a negative presence. Sometimes I felt that the mere sight of me, or the sound of my voice, would make her recoil. The room that I had once shared with her now had a lock on the inside of the door, constantly in use.

The following December, when Ariel was home for Christmas vacation from Kenyon College, she told me one morning that she wanted to go out for dinner with me that night — just the two of us, to some place special. She said she had something she wanted to talk about.

This was unusual, since Ariel had never been a very chatty person, especially in the past five years. But I was thrilled and made a reservation at a wonderful place called Starfish.

At 8:00 p.m., we were sitting across from each other with a

bottle of white wine (she looked 21), having a glass before the appetizers arrived. She was very relaxed, and talking a blue streak about dozens of topics — her new boyfriend, grades, what it was like, being away at school — when suddenly she introduced a taboo subject. Hodgkin's.

"I realize how much you did for me, Mommy, when I was sick, and I wanted to thank you. I know you were there round the clock, and I know how hard it was for you, too."

"Ariel," I broke in, trying my damnedest not to totally embarrass her by bursting into tears in a public place, "that is the most wonderful thing you could ever tell me, but no thank-yous are necessary. I did what I needed to do, because you are more precious to me than anything else on earth and I did not expect or need to be thanked. My one hope was that I could be a true source of comfort to you, so you would never feel alone, that you would know someone was with you in the middle, the darkest part, of the night."

She looked at me and smiled.

"Mommy, I know that you were with me, in the same room, sitting next to my bed, or even on my bed. But I also knew — from the age of eleven, when I was first diagnosed — that I was alone. Especially if and when you die, you let go, and go alone."

Her words were so sincere and so profound, they left me speechless. Some little voice inside my heart was protesting vehemently, saying, "No, darling, no, that is simply not true! Love can cross all boundaries, even the one between life and death!" but this was the one time that I remained quiet. I knew no matter what I said, I could not convince her, or change her mind.

I began to wonder if she were not convincing me. Maybe she had seen the truth, and my Pollyana version was the illusion.

But the more I thought about it, the more I realized that she was entitled to her version, just as I was entitled to mine, and we could respect each other's truths, even if we couldn't share them.

At that moment, I knew that at last, on both sides, a healthy separation had occurred.

After all, two first persons singular do make up one first person plural.

October 7, 1998, *Villa Spanocchia*, Italy

Three Generations of Feminists

WHEN I WAS GROWING up, my mother Millie was always president of some woman's organization or other, contributing her best efforts toward equal education, equal pay, and equal rights. She was so respected, in fact, that she was asked to write *The Feminine Mystique,* before Betty Friedan. She accepted this assignment and, for about three months, whenever dinner was over (whether it was family dinner, a restaurant dinner with friends, or one of the weekly dinner parties that she and my father hosted at home), she would plunk her Smith Corona typewriter down on the end of the dining room table along with a pack of Salems and type and chain smoke until two or three in the morning.

Then one day, she stopped.

The typewriter went away and the dining room didn't smell like smoke every morning. It might have been because she was not a natural writer, or because she didn't have the time required for research and interviews, or because she felt unqualified to be the voice of her — and future — generations of women.

It probably was a combination. While I was a little sorry that she wouldn't be writing this groundbreaking book, I was also relieved that Betty Friedan — a well-respected journalist and activist — would write it, instead. She posited that for women, as well as for men, "identity was largely cultivated through a sense of personal achievement, primarily through a career." One of the pivotal books of my generation, *The Feminine Mystique* became an international best seller and Friedan became known as "the mother of the modern women's movement."

That's a big responsibility. One which I don't think Millie was prepared to handle. And I think I understand why.

First of all, she maintained the appearance of a traditional 'fifties wife and mother. She'd been engaged at seventeen, married at eighteen, and graduated from college at nineteen. This was possible because she was very smart, had skipped three grades, and entered NYU at fifteen. Millie's father, Grandpa Sam, insisted on one condition before he would bestow his blessing on Lou Robbins, his future son-in-law: Millie had to graduate from college. Lou agreed. Millie took her textbooks on her honeymoon and graduated the following year. When asked why she married so young, she confessed it was to get out of the house, where her parents frowned on her leftist political leanings.

As a corollary to her traditional role of wife, Millie never challenged my father's refusal to let her get a paying job. In the 'fifties, this reflected badly on the husband, as if they needed the second salary to make ends meet. But she figured out a way around this, throwing herself into volunteer work on a grand scale. Her obituary, which appeared in *The New York Times* on

May 9, 2011, was written by staff editor David Slotnick, who interviewed several of her colleagues, along with my sister and me. It had a large photo, took up several columns, and cited such impressive positions as:

- 1948: One of the Founders of United Cerebral Palsy; ran their telethon, was the first President of their Women's Division. At the time, she was twenty-six; I was one and my sister was five.
- 1957-1964: UN Representative for the National Council of Women of the US (co-founded by Susan B. Anthony in 1888, this is the oldest nonsectarian women's organization in America.)
- 1964-1968: President of the National Council of Women of the USA; organized the first Women's Conference on National Service.
- 1968-1970: Vice President of the International Council of Women, worked with the US Office of Economic Opportunity.
- 1968-1974: Participated in the development of the International Peace Academy.
- 1978: Organized an International Task Force of Women, and served as a member of the US Delegation, preparing a resolution focused on women in science and technology.

That was just the beginning. In 1979, she co-founded The Trickle Up Program with her second husband, Glen Leet, which was to receive commendations from three US

Presidents. The list of her awards and honorary degrees for the following thirty-two years would take up the next two pages.

But what is relevant here were the early years, while Jane and I were young. My mother and Ms. Friedan were, after all, early members of the second wave of feminism, furthering the cause led by Susan B. Anthony and Elizabeth Cady Stanton, who founded the National Women's Suffrage Association in 1869.

Aside from the obvious similarity, that they both headed national organizations (Ms. Friedan started the National Organization of Women, a more radical group than the National Council of Women) they shared one other subtle trait: Both managed to keep husband and children in the background to protect their feminist image.

Social historian Daniel Horowitz, in *Betty Friedan and the Making of The Feminine Mystique* (1998), revealed that "Friedan had been dishonest about her vantage point, which she claimed was that of a suburban mother and housewife. She had been a leftist radical activist from the time she was at Smith College." It was, he concluded, "a necessary fiction if both she and her feminist ideas were to be given a chance to take root."

So they both had to compartmentalize their personal lives, although it was clear that work was their priority. The result was mixed messages to my sister and me, since we saw that our mother was devoting her life to liberating women, but she didn't strike us as particularly liberated herself. On the one hand, she was totally dedicated to her cause and worked an eighty-hour week. On the other hand, she was struggling to play the role of a traditional wife, daughter, and daughter-in-law. Okay, so she fell short on the role of mother. Something had to give. But for many years, she managed to keep up different personae for her different audiences.

Here are two very clear examples.

She always attended — and often hosted — social events with my father. Although he was patronizing about her career, referring to her as "a do-gooder," he also was proud of her and impressed by the circles that she traveled in: socialites from the philanthropic organizations, ambassadors from the UN. She was a fourth generation New Yorker, who — on her mother's side — came from wealth and taste. She was smart, articulate, and attractive. She was a social asset.

No matter when she woke up (usually 5:30 a.m.), or how many hours she put in at work, she was always ready for an evening out with my father. And she hosted their weekly dinner parties for twelve, to entertain his clients and friends. Of course, it helped that we had a cook so, although she created the menu and occasionally went to the supermarket, Millie didn't have to do any cooking, serving, or cleanup. Also impressive, she hosted Lou's parents for Shabbat dinner every Friday night.

Not that she was in the least religious. Having grown up in an Orthodox, Kosher household, she couldn't wait to cast that life aside when she got married. But she respected her husband's and in-laws' religious beliefs (Reformed), so always made it home on time on Friday. She also invariably complimented Grandma Esther on her Gefilte fish, made from live carp which had been swimming in her bathtub the day before.

But the most telling example is this one: As a high-profile leader of the National Council of Women who'd been outspoken on civil rights, Millie was invited to stand on the podium with Martin Luther King when he gave his *I Have a Dream* speech at the Lincoln Memorial, on August 28, 1963 in Washington DC. I was sixteen at the time, a junior in high school. I have a photograph that documents her presence, standing among the twenty or so people near him.

In the summer of 2013, to mark the fiftieth anniversary of his famous speech, a reporter from *The Washington Post* was

writing a story about the people who'd stood on the podium with Dr. King that day. The reporter managed to identify most of them, including my mother, whom she learned had died two years before. When she contacted me and asked what I remembered about my mother's participation in that historic event, my answer wasn't the story she was expecting, but it was the truth. What I remembered was that my mother didn't tell anyone in our family where she was going that day. She left early in the morning and somehow managed to get back to New York in time for Shabbat dinner that night.

Although Millie had just witnessed one of the great moments in American civil rights history that day, she didn't say a word about it over dinner. Her husband and his parents would have disapproved. In fact, if she had told them in advance, they might very well have forbidden her to go, worrying that it wasn't safe. So she just left without telling anyone where she was going. Not the behavior of a rabid feminist. It wasn't until eight years later, after my father had died, that I learned about her participation in that great day. Later, she was enormously proud of having been there, and displayed the photo on the baby grand piano in the living room for the rest of her life.

So, growing up, I was confused. On the one hand, I constantly heard her idealistic views about women fulfilling their potential and effecting positive change; on the other, I saw a woman who sat down to dinner with her in-laws every Friday night, and had to sneak off to a history-changing political event.

I was further confused by my father and his dreams for his daughters' futures. He was a first-generation Russian Jew who had managed to transform himself into a sophisticated, urbane, successful lawyer and deal-maker. The poster child for assimilation and upward mobility, he had changed his family name from Rabbinowitz, which means "Son of a Rabbi," to the far more neutral Robbins. (There were eleven generations of Rabbis in our family in Russia.) Millie couldn't have cared less about social status, but she contributed to her husband's success because that was part of her role as a good wife.

Lou was charming and charismatic, remarkable given his joyless upbringing. He could make anyone laugh and people who met him were quick to welcome him into their social circle and, ultimately, into their lives. This was a man who had gone to public schools and put himself through law school at night during the Depression. He'd started his own law firm and, in a short time, became successful, both professionally and socially.

When it came to his children, he wanted us to get the best education possible, both in and out of school. He imbued in us a love of the arts, of food and wine, of travel, and of languages. But he didn't necessarily want us to do anything with these skills. At different times during high school, although I expressed interest in both law and medicine, he didn't take either of those careers very seriously. (Nor, surprisingly, did Millie.) His greatest desire was to have his daughters marry successful men who could continue to give us the lifestyle that he had worked so hard to provide. "You never have to worry," he told us repeatedly, "you will always have someone to take care of you." The implication was, *I have brought up intelligent, cultured young ladies, who don't have to go out and get a high-pressure, high-paying job; your husbands will provide for you. And I will also leave something for you.*

No wonder Jane and I chose impractical careers, both enthusiastically supported by my father: Jane was going to be an actress, I was going to be an opera singer. Neither of which would provide a reliable source of income. On some unconscious level, he must have thought, *How great; by supporting their careers, I will be a patron of the arts!*

I was a senior in college when my father had his first heart attack. He was in Egypt, having eaten and drunk his way across Africa, despite his doctor's recent warning that he had arteriosclerosis and was at risk of a heart attack or stroke. During the month he spent in an Egyptian hospital, he lost sixty pounds. When he finally returned home, I almost didn't recognize him.

He had grown a bushy mustache to conceal his skeletal frame. His collar bones protruded and his ribs stuck out. This was a shadow of the convivial host and raconteur I'd grown up with; the man who loved to entertain, to eat, to drink, to make people laugh, and who'd dreamed of owning his own restaurant.

He survived for a year on a strict diet that deprived him of all of his favorite foods, including even the use of salt, which seriously affected his quality of life. Plus, he lived in dreaded anticipation of the next heart attack. When it finally happened, I suspected his anxiety had brought it on. He died when I was twenty-one, the year I graduated from college, and his loss left me with many unresolved issues. He was overprotective and when my sister or I did something of which he disapproved, his fits of rage could be terrifying. For many years, I couldn't deal with anger and didn't dare challenge a man in a position of authority.

The day of his funeral, my then-boyfriend Mel moved in with my then-best-friend, Mimi. I could barely process my father's death, much less their betrayal. My first term at NYU graduate school was ending and I had to get extensions on all my papers because, for weeks, I could do nothing but lie in bed and listen to Beethoven quartets while following the scores.

My father had despised my new boyfriend Mel, who represented everything that he objected to in a potential suitor for his daughter. Like my father, Mel was a first-generation Russian Jew, raised in Brooklyn, whose parents spoke with an accent. But that's where their similarities ended. He was a teacher (granted, at Stuyvesant, one of the best public schools in the city); he had long curly blond hair that crept over his collar, and he wore blue jeans. I don't know if he even owned a suit. Mel was a good teacher but money didn't interest him and he was totally lacking in ambition. In fact, he was happiest getting stoned and lying around his fourth-floor walkup off First Avenue. I might as well have told my father we were moving back to Brooklyn, which he prided himself on having escaped thirty years earlier.

The day of the funeral, in Mel and Mimi's conspicuous absence, I wish I could have told him, *Oh boy, Dad, you were so right.*

So when I was introduced to another young man by a good friend of my father's, it was as if the universe had thrown me a life ring. This new candidate, astoundingly, was about the same height and weight as my father; he even wore the same size suit (forty-two L), and was enamored of British bespoke clothing, especially Turnbull & Asser shirts. David had gone to all the right private schools — Trinity and Penn — then law school at Boston University. He worked in a bank and wanted to be a millionaire before he was thirty. The contrast with Mel was blinding, but these surface details were to prove misleading.

I had gone to a psychiatrist after my father's death, in order to spur myself out of my catatonic grief. When I described my quickly developing dependence on my new boyfriend, Dr. Bauer would peer over his bifocals and say, "Red light. Red light!" I ignored his warnings.

Two years later we were married. And two years after that, I slapped a *New Yorker* cartoon onto the fridge with a magnet. Under the "Just Married" sign taped to the back window of car with cans streaming behind it, was a smaller sign reading, "For all the Wrong Reasons."

I pursued my career as a fledgling opera singer, which he found glamorous at first, then inconvenient. I wasn't part of a major opera company and my gigs were at least a month or two apart, but rehearsals and performances were at night, which meant I couldn't always be home to cook dinner for him or his friends and clients. Plus, he wanted me to bring in an income. The idea of the husband being the sole source of support of a family had become old-fashioned by then. So I took part-time jobs, working at Drama Bookshop Publishers, as a journalist and, eventually, in a PR firm.

Then I gave birth to a beautiful, perfect daughter, Ariel. Just a few months into my joyous new role as mother, I became increasing unhappy. Whether this was due to post-partum mood swings or the sullen, non-helpful behavior of my husband, who resented my shift of attention from him to the baby, I don't know. But everything I did annoyed him and we fought constantly. I had outgrown the role of husband's handmaiden and five years into the marriage, even though I had a toddler, I was finally able to stand up for myself and knew I had to get out.

It was scary to think of being a single parent and of being alone. But it was even more scary to stay in a relationship that was constricting, forcing me to be someone I wasn't. Or wasn't anymore. And I couldn't see raising a child with someone whose values and philosophy of life were poles apart from my own.

Perhaps I had outgrown the need to please my father. Perhaps now it was time to please my mother. Oh hell, let's be honest. It was time to please myself.

It was a relief to be on my own and the transition to single mother was a lot easier than I'd feared. Still bearing the scars of Millie's absence while I was young, I refused to get a full-time job until Ariel was in kindergarten. It was my chance to re-write mother-daughter history. I continued to work part-time, as a freelance journalist and for a PR agency.

When Ariel entered kindergarten, I had a carefully prepared talk with her.

"Mommy is going to be working full-time starting on Monday, so I won't be home when you get home, but Paula will be there, and I'm just a phone call away; I can be here in ten minutes."

"Uh-huh" she said, barely listening.

I raced home from my first day at the full-time job.

"Darling," I yodeled from the doorway as I slammed the front door open. "Mommy's home! Oh, I missed you so much…"

Ariel was sitting on my bed watching Sesame Street. She didn't move. Didn't even turn her head around. She just said "Shhh. I'm watching this."

Another transition, far easier than I had expected.

One job led to another. With each one, I became a little more ambitious, a little more competitive, a little more confident, so I wasn't surprised when, in my forties, I started my own company with a partner. At first, I chastised myself. What took me so long? But by that time, Ariel was in college and my time was my own. Considering how all-consuming it was to run my own business, I realize I couldn't have done it before, nor would I have wanted to. She was my priority.

I think of myself as having been in a transitional generation.

I was acutely aware of women's liberation and a proud charter subscriber to *Ms. Magazine*. But most of my contemporaries had also received mixed messages from their parents, so it wasn't surprising that I hadn't "self-realized" until I was almost halfway through my life.

I think the third generation's the charm. Ariel never questioned that she would have a career, it was a given. She started working in retail at sixteen. Her school constantly reinforced the importance being productive in life. I had attended the same school and heard the same message. But the cultural context of the '50s and '60s was a far cry from that of the '80s and '90s.

I regard my daughter's accomplishments with awe. She is tremendously capable, independent, driven. She works long hours at her job, spends holidays with her husband's parents up in Boston, never misses a dance recital or a parent-teacher conference, and socializes with the parents of Sage's friends. My parents didn't know my *own* friends throughout my thirteen years at Brearley, much less their parents.

While the fight for equal pay and opportunities continues, I think we've covered a lot of ground in three generations. And I know that my granddaughter Sage will have an even easier time of it. Thanks to people like Betty and Bella and Gloria.

And Millie.

This past Mother's Day, Ariel posted the photograph of her grandmother standing on the podium near Dr. King on Instagram. She proudly showed it to Sage explaining the goals to which her great-grandmother had dedicated her life. Ariel was right, Millie is an inspiring role model. In different ways, her accomplishments are as extraordinary as those of Betty Friedan's. Ms. Friedan's book may have sold millions of copies, but Millie's work helped to change well over a million women's lives in practical and concrete ways. Here's the opening quote from the home page of the Trickle Up Organization that Millie and Glen founded:

Since 1979, Trickle Up has helped 335,000 women gain the skills and confidence to achieve greater economic self-sufficiency. When women succeed, so can their children and families. Since five people on average benefit for each woman we reach, we've helped over 1.5 million people total. In the next five years, we're committed to helping the next million graduates out of extreme poverty.

Ariel was asked to be one of the introductory speakers at Trickle Up's Fortieth Anniversary Gala on April 8th this year. She was honored to accept.

January 2019

The desire to get married is a basic and primal instinct in women. It's followed by another basic and primal instinct: the desire to be single again.

~ *Nora Ephron*

IV

Relationships

Laughter is not at all a bad beginning for a friendship,
and it is far the best ending.

~ *Oscar Wilde*

With my dear friends Peter Kazaras and Armin Baier, who I consider family, at Ariel's wedding in 2005.

My husband Alex Berger with our spaniels, William and Henry, at our house in Hillsdale, NY.

Protective Spells

DUE TO IRRECONCILABLE DIFFERENCES, confirmed by our marriage counselor and our lawyers, my first husband and I were going through a divorce. It was not amicable. We had different values and different priorities. And more importantly, I was never going to be able to keep as clean a house as his mother.

Before he moved out, there was a little stretch of time when we continued to share the same bedroom and the same bed. This made for many sleepless nights on my part because I was afraid of physical harm (he was 6'3" and about 215 pounds). In my mind, there was a dotted line drawn down the center of the bed, and if any of my limbs even accidentally fell over that line, in my paranoid fantasies, he would reach down for the machete that he was hiding under his side of the bed and lop off the errant limb. This physical fear for my life, although irrational, was based on an incident which occurred a few weeks earlier, on New Year's Eve. Right before we left for a party, he pulled a Saturday night special out of the top shelf of the hall coat closet and pointed it at me. As I discovered later, it was a plastic toy gun, and he thought it was amusing; but at the time, it sure looked real to me.

My daughter was two-and-a-half at the time and attending All Soul's Nursery School on 80th Street and Lexington Avenue. As the semester wore on, when I dropped her off, I was looking progressively exhausted and stressed. One day, Stefan, one of the fathers at this proper Upper East Side nursery school, asked me if I were okay. He himself was separated and had custody of his very adorable bowl-cut blond toddler.

"No, not really," I replied with uncharacteristic honesty, too tired to pretend. "I'm going through a difficult divorce, and not getting much sleep; I feel like I am in danger in my own home."

"That's terrible," he said. "I understand. I think I have something that could help you."

"That would be great. I'm pretty desperate right now, I'm ready to try anything," I replied.

"I've been seeing Maria Gonzalez, a Santera — a priestess of Santería." He further explained that it was a mystical religious practice that African slaves brought to the Caribbean which combines African, Native Indian, and Roman Catholic traditions.

"She's from Puerto Rico and doesn't speak much English but has a large and devoted following in the Hispanic community. She works out of her home in the Bronx. She has spells to protect you."

"Might be tricky," I said. "I understand Spanish, but I don't speak it very well, and I also have no idea how to get anywhere in the Bronx. I'd be scared to death to try to find her house by myself."

"Not to worry. I could take you there. I speak Spanish, so I could translate for you. We just take the subway to Morrison Avenue, and then a bus to Randall Avenue. It takes about an hour."

"Is it safe?" I queried, having only been to the Bronx to visit the Zoo, and having no idea how welcoming the ethnic community might be to an Upper East Side Caucasian.

"I've gone a number of times, never had a problem," he said. "I think we should go soon. How's Friday morning?"

"Hmmm…Friday…yes, hmmm…fine," I said, trying to sound enthusiastic or at least convinced that I would come back alive from this little field trip to the Bronx not to mention the spirit world with a divorced father whom I only knew superficially from chatting with him after dropping my daughter off.

"Then it's settled," he said. "I'll call her and make an appointment for ten."

"Okay. I'll arrange for my babysitter to pick my daughter up from school, and set up a play date. Thank you so much, Stefan. I really appreciate your help." I felt a little wave of relief, since I believed that this priestess really could help.

Friday morning, after we dropped off our kids at All Souls, we got on the number six train on 77th Street and Lex. It was a long ride, and then we had to wait for the bus, but he knew the way, so at least I didn't have to have a total panic attack about getting lost.

We arrived at her apartment building a little early, so we

had to wait in the antechamber. That in itself was daunting. There was a statuette of the Virgin on an altar, made out of a few steps covered in dark velvet, all spookily lit by flickering candles. I was wondering if closing the door too hard would cause a wind that would make the candle flames catch the velvet, setting the room instantly on fire. I double-checked the location of the front door. Part of me thought, *This is nuts, I should just walk back out the door while there's still time.* And another part of me thought, *This is great, it's the real thing, I know this will help.*

About fifteen minutes later, the Santera opened the door to her inner sanctum to let out a young Hispanic man. She was an older woman, with a heavily wrinkled face and fly-away white hair. She had a fringed shawl around her shoulders and looked straight out of central casting. I quelled another moment of panic as I walked into her room, which had even more statues of the Virgin, more candles, and lots of brain-fogging incense. It was quite dark and the candles cast eerie shadows on the walls.

Stefan came with me. I could understand most of what she said, but had trouble communicating my concerns, so he told her that I needed a spell for protection, since I was in danger.

She nodded, sagely. "It is your husband who wishes you harm," she said in Spanish, adding, "There are bad spirits throughout your house. I will pray for you now, but you must cleanse yourself and your entire home. You have to perform certain rituals and exorcise the evil spirits in all the rooms."

She spent about ten minutes reciting prayers in a mixture of Spanish and Latin. Then she went over to a sideboard and put several ingredients into a large plastic spray bottle, like the kind Windex comes in. They included some type of holy water, rose water, a holy oil, and a mix of herbs — the only one I distinctly remember is myrrh, since it was so unusual and sounded so Biblical.

After she finished praying, she gave me the following instructions. It was important to follow them exactly, she said. As soon as I got home, I was to fill a bathtub with hot water, spray some of the holy water around the edges, strew the petals of white flowers on the water, and then submerge myself totally for at least ten minutes. Then, late at night when everyone was asleep, I should take the bottle and spray every corner of every room.

I think she charged all of $25 for the consultation and the holy water.

As I walked out of her apartment, I found I could breathe more easily and my stress headache was beginning to disappear. On my way home, I stopped off at a local florist and bought an armful of white flowers.

There was no-one home, thank heavens. I immediately drew a bath, sprayed the holy mixture around the edges, and then spent ten minutes plucking petals off the dozens of white flowers until the entire surface of the water was covered with them.

I got into the tub and was almost completely submerged when the door to my bathroom opened and Paula, the babysitter from Trinidad, walked in and screamed at the top of her lungs.

"Oh, Ms. Robbins! Do you know what are you doing?

You are calling on spirits! This is dangerous. I can't be around this."

Shaking her head and waving her hands in the air, she ran out of the bathroom. I was not going to be deterred from following the Santera's instructions to the letter, however, so I stayed submerged for about ten minutes.

As soon as she saw me leave the bathroom, Paula, who had been standing near the front door with her coat on, stalked out. Which was fine, since I was looking forward to spending the rest of the afternoon with my daughter.

Later that night, when I was sure my husband was fast asleep, I crept out of bed. It was around 2:00 a.m. I took my bottle of holy water and, starting at the far end of the house, sprayed the kitchen, the dining room, the hallway, and finally made my way into the living room.

I stood up on the upholstered arm of the pink velvet couch against the far wall and started spritzing wildly. As I was leaping from one arm of the couch to the other, I suddenly saw a dark shape materialize in the doorway.

"What the *hell* are you doing?" said my husband in a loud voice.

I had one of those deer-in-the-headlights moments, when my brain froze and I couldn't think of any rational explanation. The first thing that shot out of my mouth was,

"It's my last-ditch effort to save our marriage. I'm *cleaning!*"

My husband shook his head and went back into the bedroom. I took my time spraying the living room, and then quietly climbed into my half of the bed. Thinking he was now sharing his bed with a lunatic, he had left me extra room, so

I didn't have to sleep clinging to the edge of the mattress as I usually did. It's working, I thought.

Buenas noches y gracias, I murmured.

March 1981

Cartier Takes it Back

GEORGE AND I WERE having the same argument we'd been having for years. But this time, I was so frustrated and angry that when I slammed my wine glass down on the table of an expensive French restaurant, the stem snapped and I was left holding a bowl full of red wine, some of which splashed all over the ivory linen tablecloth.

I handed the top half of the wine glass to the waiter, who rushed over when he saw the glass break. I grabbed my pocketbook, stormed out of the restaurant, jumped into a cab, and sped home.

George and I were both unhappily married when we had first met; I was in couples' therapy with my then husband and had already spoken to a lawyer about a divorce. So, even though it would be complicated, George and I promised to divorce our respective spouses and marry each other as soon as we could. Within a year, at great expense — both financial and emotional — I was divorced, but he was not.

"I can't get divorced now, the timing is wrong," he'd say. "I've worked so hard to build my company, I would have to dismantle it and sell off most of my assets. She will do anything she can to ruin me. Just give me time to hide more of my assets." And then the oft-heard refrain, "But know that I love you and want to spend the rest of my life with you." He called me every morning when he woke up, and every night before he went to sleep, constantly reassuring me of his undying love.

The sad part was, I knew that both his recalcitrance to go through a fortune-draining divorce and his love for me were equally strong. No clear winner.

So I waited. At first, he said six months, maybe a year. But before I knew it, two years had passed, then five, then seven. Instead of working towards hiding any assets, he continued to build his empire: grain all over the Midwest, silos, barges on the Mississippi, railroads. I felt as if I were watching him play Monopoly. He told me about every new acquisition, and how the consummation of each deal was a rush, completely addictive. He also taught me about the art of negotiation: you had to be willing to risk it all, "to throw the keys down on the table and walk away." It was a lesson that would come in handy.

But after seven years, I wasn't getting any younger. I had wanted to have more children; and was it asking so much for us to live under the same roof and hear his late-night declarations of love on the pillow, not over the phone?

The phone. Yes, the night I broke the wine glass, he called. I let it ring and ring, never picked up. It was over.

The next day, I took my usual route home from the headquarters of Campari USA, across 52nd Street, past Cartier's flagship store on Fifth. I loved looking in the windows. Which is how I happened to spot my necklace, the one George had given me about a year ago, along with a set of keys to a country house which never materialized.

It was one of the very few pieces that Cartier has ever produced which I honestly thought was ugly. It was a figa, an ancient charm that was supposed to ward off evil spirits, in the shape of a hand, lopped off below the wrist, with the thumb tightly tucked between the second and third fingers.

This in itself was not terrible, but there was a black pearl jammed in the palm of the hand as well. The amulet was hanging from an 18K gold chain. He usually had fairly good taste, so when he first gave it to me, I thought he might have sent his secretary to pick it out (this, in the days when people still had secretaries).

I took the figa-sighting, the day after our fight, as a sign.

That night as soon as I got home, I went straight to the top drawer of my bureau, and pulled out the rectangular red leather, gold-tooled Cartier box.

I opened it, and sure enough, there was the gold figa, clutching the ugly black pearl. I put it in my shoulder bag.

The next day, on my way home from the office, I checked out the same window on the 52nd Street side. Yup, the necklace was still there.

I strode purposefully into the store, quickly scanning the room for the most appropriate salesperson to approach. Aha. Found her. A young, slender, innocent-looking girl.

She saw me walking towards her and said, "May I help you, Madame?" in a deferential, quiet voice. Perfect.

"Yes, thank you so much," I replied. "I have a little gift I'd like to exchange." I reached into my bag, extracted the pristine Cartier box, and placed it on the glass vitrine in front of her. "It's the figa that's in your window," I said, opening the box. There it was in all of its hideous glory, as shiny as the day it was purchased.

"I've never worn it. My boyfriend gave it to me for my birthday, but it's really not me, and I was hoping to exchange it for something that I could wear every day."

"Of course," she said, smiling brightly, "I'd be happy to help you. Why don't you look around and find something you'd prefer?" And she gave me the price.

Talk about a kid in a candy store. I circumnavigated the floor, avoiding the really expensive stuff, and concentrated on the more casual pieces before I ended up back at her counter.

"All I need from you is the purchase slip," she said.

"Oh dear," I answered, looking flustered. "I don't have the sales slip — it was a gift, and I never would have asked him for the receipt, since I didn't want him to know I was returning it, certainly not two days after he gave it to me."

"Ok, don't worry," she said, "I can always look up the sale in the recent invoices."

"That would be great!" I said enthusiastically.

She went over to a beautiful leather desk, and extracted a large leather-bound folder. "You say he bought it recently?" she asked.

"Well, my birthday was on Saturday," I began, not mentioning that the Saturday in question was a year ago, "and he always waits until the last minute to buy my gift..." I gave her his name and address and said he probably put it on his Platinum American Express card.

After several minutes of thumbing through a large packet of purchase slips, she said, "You know, we have a thirty-day exchange policy, and I've just gone through the past thirty days, but I am *so* sorry. I don't see it."

I looked puzzled and upset, and started rubbing my fingers over my temples. "Oh, please don't get upset" she immediately said, "I can go back sixty or even ninety days." She started flipping through a larger group of invoices.

A little while later, she looked up with a baleful expression. "I am so terribly sorry, Madame, I can't seem to find it."

I continued massaging my temples, as if warding off an incipient migraine. "I don't understand," I murmured, "unless he bought it before he met me, for someone else. He was seeing someone else when we met. That must be it."

I paused and took a deep breath. "Please stop looking," I said. "I don't want the necklace. Nor do I want to exchange it. I am going to leave it right here, on this counter. I never want to see it or George ever again."

I buttoned my coat, flung my bag over my shoulder and started to walk towards the front door. I had taken about four steps when I heard her running behind me and felt her hand on my arm. "Madame, please don't go!" she pleaded. "Of course I'll take it back. You know what the amount of your credit is, try to find something you like."

"That is so terribly kind of you, "I said quietly, trying to sound as if I were fighting back tears when in fact I was fighting a wide grin. I forced myself to walk slowly to the case where I had seen the three-colored gold hoop earrings that I coveted. She followed at a respectful distance. I sighed, and looked distractedly at the contents of the case in front of me. "I suppose I might as well just try on those simple gold earrings," I finally managed to croak out.

"It would be my pleasure," she said, getting the key that unlocked the vitrine. She pulled the earrings out and placed them on a tray lined with black velvet which made them pop dramatically. I slowly reached over to the tray and picked them up. I put them back on the tray, removed my own insignificant pearl earrings, and tried on the gold hoops. They were drop-dead gorgeous.

"I guess they're all right," I muttered, half to myself. "You know, they cheer me up; I think I'll just wear them out, if I may."

"Wonderful idea, let me get you the right box for them." She ducked under the counter and came up with another red leather box, into which she put my pearl earrings which looked drab and old fashioned, and which I wouldn't want to be caught dead wearing.

"You look so beautiful in them, I'm sure they'll bring you good luck," she said. "And you will find someone much better than George."

"I think you're right," I said, going for a despondent-but-hopeful look. "And may I thank you so very much for your extraordinary help."

And, I thought, *thank you George, for teaching me the art of negotiation.*

August 1980

Travels with Nathan

AUGUST 2, 1989: AFTER about a year of silence, my old friend Nate calls and invites me away for the weekend. To my delight, he makes it clear that this weekend is *on him*. He's willing to fly up to New York from Miami, where he moved twelve years ago to be near his aging parents. I accept immediately, since that was one of the occasional weekends when my ex-husband was taking my eleven-year-old daughter and I always felt bereft when she was gone. "Great," I said, "it's been too long — can't wait to catch up in person!"

August 13: Nate tells me that he's booked a Friday afternoon flight that will put him in New York by dinner time. After conferring with him, I make a reservation at *La Boîte en Bois*.

August 16, 1:00 p.m.: Nate calls me at the office to say he *just* looked at the ticket from his travel agent and discovered he is booked on a *7:00 p.m.* flight out of Miami, so he won't arrive in New York until around 10:30. The hairs stand up at the back of my neck as I flash back twenty-four years ago. I was a senior in high school and had just been introduced to Nate; his mother was the best friend of one of my mother's best friends. On our second date, I waited for him for an hour in the pouring rain in front of a chic little French bistro, *Le Boeuf* à *la Mode*. When I arrived, to my dismay, I discovered that the restaurant had closed. When Nate finally arrived, instead of apologizing, he got angry at me for being dumb enough to stand out in the rain for such a long time.

Since he was basically an old family friend and I also wondered why I was dumb enough to wait so long in the rain, I forgave him. Although I wasn't interested in him romantically, he was fun to spend time with, since he was smart, had a great sense of humor, knew a lot about wine and food and, to a senior in high school, seemed very worldly — he was already a practicing lawyer and was bilingual (his mother, although Polish by birth, grew up in Paris).

So I decide it's not *déjà vu* all over again, it's just a coincidence.

7:30 p.m.: Nate calls to tell me that his Pan Am flight to La Guardia has been canceled, but that he can probably catch an 8 p.m. flight to Newark. I try to sound upbeat, although I am already exhausted and my suspicions creep back. I'm sure a snack will help.

11:45 p.m.: Have fallen asleep with a book on my chest when the doorman rings up to announce Nate's arrival. Ever the gracious hostess, I offer to make him something to eat. (After canceling our dinner reservation, my own hasty meal consisted of a peanut butter and honey sandwich on challah toast.) He declines my offer, explaining that he can't eat right before he goes to bed. He then launches into a litany of hypochondriacal complaints, from a sensitive stomach (incipient ulcers?) to the recent presence of a protruding bone in his right hand (arthritis?).

He is exhausted too, so with some degree of self-consciousness and modesty, we crawl into my queen-size bed together. I am wearing the long-sleeved floor-length white nightgown that Brook's daughter Brett bought me as a house gift. Nate has stripped down to his white undershirt and jockey shorts. We manage to get to sleep, chastely, around 1 a.m., after taking Halcyon, a powerful sleeping pill, which just so happened to have been *Newsweek's* cover story that week. Nate remarks that the drug, if taken in quantity, can destroy entire memory banks, which immediately compels me to check if I can recall my home address and telephone number.

Saturday, August 17: We wake up five hours later when Oliver the spaniel walks across Nate's chest and curls himself around my head. I assumed we would sleep for seven hours or more, given the strength of the drug. Was this worth wiping out ninth grade Latin and Greek? Oh well, I have to get up and get dressed, since Cammie is coming to pick up the dog any minute and will board him for the rest of the weekend.

We now have to find a place to stay for Saturday night, rent a car, pack, and leave the city. After several phone calls, Nate finally chances on a small bed and breakfast in Cold Spring, right on the Hudson River near Garrison. It sounds ideal, at least judging from the enthusiasm of the man on the phone. One more brief phone call and Nate has rented a car.

Everything seems to be moving along at a brisk clip until I start to pack. But let me back up for a moment to report that Nate's first comment upon walking into my apartment and seeing me for the first time in a year was, "What did you do to your hair — it's *red!*" (accompanied by a grimace). Granted, my hair color has been subtly transitioning from brunette to auburn for some time now, but it's not *red* by any stretch of the imagination. Anyway, it's not as if I was going to have time to re-color my hair before we left and, more to the point, how dare he comment on my hair? What little is left of *his* hair is predominantly grey and is combed *forward,* to "fool" people into thinking that his bald spot does not extend all the way to the back of his head. Right, like that always works.

Oh, never mind, I'm just being vindictive. Truth be told, Nate did stop complaining about my hair long enough to make two other insightful and caring remarks about my appearance. First, he tells me I should see a dermatologist about the dark circles under my eyes, which make me look exhausted and stressed. Goodness, I thought having a child with a serious illness was my biggest problem right now. Instead, my focus all along should have been on skincare. Nate is wildly reassuring, however, pointing out that skin lightening is minor procedure, involving just a few chemicals.

Second, Nate cheerily tells me that the patterned Bermuda shorts I have chosen to wear for the trip are the most hideous item of clothing he has ever seen. The color is too bright and the cut is terrible, too long and baggy in front. No problem, I think, I'll just slip into another chic ensemble that I picked up on one of my compulsive shopping sprees.

Twenty minutes later, with sportswear separates three deep on my bed, exercycle, and floor, I finally arrive at an outfit Nate finds acceptable: white shorts and a turquoise polo shirt that

I have to steal from Ariel's bureau, having exhausted my own supply of casual shirts. And what an amazing coincidence this turns out to be, because Nate himself happens to be wearing white shorts and a purple polo shirt!

After another hour packing for a twenty-four-hour trip, we finally leave the house. We grab a bite to eat at Island, a WASP-y restaurant on 93rd and Madison. After ordering the *Vichysoisse*, cold leek and potato soup, Nate informs the waiter that he would "never trust a recipe that begins, *First, take a leek…*" Then he ominously warns the waiter that he judges the quality of a restaurant by its soup.

The soup arrives. He takes two spoonfuls and pushes it aside. For the remainder of the meal, we have a new waiter. By this time, I am beginning to question whether I can make it through the rest of the day traveling solo with him, so I suggest we visit my friend Rebecca and her husband who have a summer cottage on Lake Mahopac, right on our way.

Okay, so it was slightly out of the way, and yes, we did get lost, but that was just because Nate insisted on taking the Palisades Parkway although Rebecca had given me directions for the Taconic. After about two-and-a-half hours in the car for a trip that should have taken an hour and ten, I suggest we call them for directions. I get their answering machine, which only contributes to Nate's darkening mood. After we'd driven around the entire lake twice, I call their house again. This time, Rebecca picks up the phone and happily informs me that we are about ten yards from her house.

We visit for only an hour because, by then, it was 4:00 p.m. and we still had to check into our romantic inn, which is approximately forty-five minutes to two hours away, depending on how lost we get.

6:45 p.m. After mistaking a small ramshackle dwelling for our inn, we finally arrive at 3 Stone Road. The house is spectacular, all wooden shingles and huge picture windows with a dazzling view of the Hudson, suffused with the golden light of the impending sunset. We learn from the owner that the elegant four-bedroom house had been built six years ago as a private residence. When the owner decided it was too large, he moved to a separate property and started renting it out instead. He usually books wedding parties but, this particular weekend, the wedding had been canceled, so basically Nate and I have the house to ourselves.

We change in a flash to make our seven-thirty reservation at a restaurant that, under the best of circumstances, is a good half-hour away. According to the owner, "The Bird & Bottle is right up Route 9–you can't miss it."

Right. Nate turns onto Route 9-D instead of Route 9 so, after about forty minutes, we find ourselves at the Bear Mountain Bridge, which is about fifteen minutes from Rebecca's house. We are so desperate by this point that we actually drive across the bridge to ask the man in the toll booth on the other side for directions but, of course, he has never heard of this eighteenth century three-star restaurant that charges fifty dollars per person (astronomical in 1989).

Retracing our route, we manage to find a gas station, but the attendant informs us that "I'm not from this country," so he hasn't heard of it either. We then turn into *another* restaurant to ask their valet parking attendant. Before we reach him, however,

I notice a sign saying *Blind Person Parking* which makes me laugh so hard that when I roll down my window to ask directions, I am wheezing and crying and am unable to speak. Nate screams the question out the window over my head. The parking attendant gives us clear directions.

9:00 p.m.: We pull into The Bird & Bottle. By a stroke of good fortune, they have not erased our name from the reservation book plus are still serving dinner. As soon as we are seated, the waiter comes over to the table and starts to list the specials of the evening; he gets as far as the "cold leek and potato soup," and I start to laugh hysterically again. Nate is mystified. "It's just hunger," I tell him.

We make it through dinner which has me on the edge of my seat, since Nate is channeling Mimi Sheraton, rating each dish and all of its ingredients in stentorian tones. I would have felt a lot better if we had ordered a decent bottle of wine, but Nate's fantasy ulcer is acting up again, so I just order a glass of California Chardonnay which he tastes and pronounces "watery, insufficiently chilled, and lacking in character."

Midnight: We find our way back to the house in record time. I look at the orangey-red harvest moon set against a night sky filled with stars and sigh. The scene is picture-book romantic but, unfortunately, my feelings for Nate have always fallen into the Platonic category. Then it occurs to me that he might be expecting something else from me; why else would he be paying for everything? So, knowing what a hypochondriac he is, I tell him that I have a little tingling on my lower lip, an area where I occasionally break out in 'fever blisters', an obvious euphemism.

From that minute on, there is no way Nate would touch me with a ten-foot pole.

The room has one double bed on a platform in the corner, peculiarly placed right next to the air conditioner. I make Nate sleep on that side. Before getting into bed, however, I suggest trying out the huge Jacuzzi in the bathroom, so we slip into the tub and let the bubbles pummel our bodies until I feel like pounded veal. While in the tub, Nate tells me all about the single life in Miami. He is now forty-eight and has never been married, which he finds inexplicable and depressing. He then explains that the women he meets (and by now, they number in the hundreds) always have fatal flaws.

Then we get to the heart of the matter. No-one measures up to his mother, a looming presence in his life. When he lived in New York City, she would visit regularly from Miami. Because she snooped around his apartment under the guise of tidying up, he had to hide his condoms in the Band-Aid box in his medicine cabinet. I begin to feel sorry for him and wish he could find someone who would make him happy. He's got so much going for him, he just has to lower his standards a little. Okay, more than a little.

Am about to faint from the heat of the Jacuzzi, so after about fifteen minutes I get out of the tub. I am sure we will drop off to sleep in an instant after the hot tub, but in fact as soon as our heads hit the pillows, we both have insomnia again. Nate can't sleep because the pillows are too firm, so he ends up taking a pillow from the couch and covering it with his undershirt. We lie in bed and chat for another hour, which is quite relaxing and reminds me of sleepovers with my best friends when I was about ten.

Just as we're beginning to get sleepy, we start to hear weird, creaky noises in the house. We immediately jump to the conclusion that the story about the canceled wedding was a total lie, and that the proprietor is an ax-murderer who preys on random guests. He waits until he thinks they're asleep and then chops them up and plants their bones in circular patterns in the driveway. At this point, we have frightened ourselves out of our wits, so we both have to take more Halcyon which immediately causes me to forget tenth and eleventh grade Latin, Greek, and French.

By now, all I want to do is curl up in my own bed with my dog. I have dozens of anxious thoughts crowding through my brain: How is Ariel? Is Cammie letting Oliver sleep on her couch? Was I going to be found dead in a bed with a man that I hadn't even slept with? Would Nate let me out of the room the next day wearing the flowered print shirt I had brought, now that the turquoise polo was dirty? And of paramount importance, what were they going to serve for breakfast?

Sunday, August 18: Even with the world-class sleeping pill, we only sleep for about five hours again. When we wake up, the Hudson is heavily shrouded in fog, which means that the minute I step out on the terrace, my hair is three inches shorter. Correction: my *ugly red* hair is three inches shorter. To make matters worse, Nate insists on taking photographs of me all around the house and lawn, with his zoom-lens Nikon.

He also insists on my taking photographs of him, but instead of letting me snap away, he gives exact instructions on where in the frame I should locate his face or body, and he pre-sets the light and distance. I, of course, give him back my own set of instructions: *Lean on the crumbling stone wall near the edge of the hill* and when he loses his balance and flails his arms, I snap away like a fiend, very Auntie Mame.

As for breakfast at this high-class B&B, I am aghast: On the side buffet table, there is a pile of pale defrosted supermarket bagels, accompanied only by a container of Philadelphia whipped cream cheese. No nova, not even jam. The coffee was made in an electric percolator. What did I expect for $200 a night? I suggest going some place for a real breakfast, but instead we decide to tour Boscobel, a prime example of Federal furniture and decorative arts. Nate thinks it's too hot to sit outdoors and have a picnic, so we decide to just head back to the city, which is fine with me.

We drive home in record time, in what I would like to think is companionable silence. Nate's head is already back in Miami and I am counting the minutes until I see my daughter and my dog.

I realize that I had had unrealistic expectations about this weekend away; I wasn't expecting romance, but I also wasn't expecting quite so many judgments. It was great to escape New York in August, and it was good to catch up with Nate, but it made me realize that he was never going to change, and since I did value his friendship, I had to accept that. He was smart, funny, and a good friend, and in smaller doses, I enjoyed his company.

August 1980

Hillsdale Journal

~I Never Lived Anywhere Below the Tenth Floor

WHEN ALEX, MY SECOND husband, was married to his first wife, they had lived in Bedford, New York. He'd loved that house with its huge flower garden, swimming pool, and large wine cellar. And he loved being in the country. Although we both worked in the city, he felt claustrophobic there. So when we got married, he wanted to have a country escape. I was enthusiastic about the idea, since I had always, *theoretically*, yearned for a house in the country. Now that it was about to become a reality, however, I was growing apprehensive. I had never lived anywhere below the tenth floor.

March 1999: Within two months, we'd both fallen in love with a house in Hillsdale, New York, close to the Massachusetts border. It was about a two-and-a-half-hour trip from the city but, as contrasted with the nightmare commute to the Hamptons, traveling to upstate New York on Route 22 or the Taconic was a beautiful drive, with little or no traffic.

Our house was perched on top of a mountain next to the Catamount Ski Area. It was a simple two-story dark wood house with a deck, but what made us gasp and grab each other's hands was the view from the floor-to-ceiling windows overlooking the Catskill mountains and the valley below. On our twelve-acre plot, there were birch trees on either side of the steep lawn, as well as maple, oak, and elm that, we were told, turned magnificent colors in the fall.

The real estate agent mentioned that the filmmakers, Merchant and Ivory, lived near us. She said they did readings in Claverack, a neighboring town. Okay, so I never caught sight of either of them, nor did I even see a flyer for one of their supposed readings, but just knowing they were nearby made me feel as if I were living in an arcane artistic community.

As much as I loved the *concept* of fresh air and being at one with nature, I was ill-prepared for country life. If anything had to be done in my Manhattan apartment, I rang on the house phone for the super or the handyman. Aside from the occasional sliver of a silverfish in the bathtub, which sent me screaming into an adjoining room, there were no bugs and no wild animals.

I got a few hints of my new environment and its wildlife when we first moved in. As we drove up to the house for the first time, I asked Alex why the grass in the front yard was matted down. "Oh," he responded casually, "that's where the deer have been sleeping."

To a naïve city-dweller, at first this sounded positively Disney-esque, but I soon realized he wasn't referring to Bambi and his mother; it was more like a herd of cloven-hoofed ruminants and, in a few months I grew to loathe this species. Not only were they Lyme-disease carriers, which affected many people in our area, but they also nibbled our flowers, vegetables, shrubs, and trees. I googled a recipe for venison jerky but later learned that it is against the law in New York State to kill deer with anything except a cross-bow and archery was never my sport.

The presence of the herd of deer might have been counterbalanced by the wild turkey hen with her line of adorable chicks which I often saw crossing our private road. That was before my first-hand experience of a wide range of small, swimming, slithering, crawling, hopping, and flying creatures. These denizens of the Hillsdale ecosystem became trapped in the swimming pool filters on a regular basis — frogs, toads, newts, lizards, large beetles — some of them winged, spiders, snakes and voles (I thought the latter existed only under "V" in children's alphabet books; I was wrong). It was like the Amazon jungle.

The first time I came across a snake coiled in the corner drain, I ran to Alex to report it with what I thought was well-muted hysteria. Alex just laughed and gave me a reassuring hug. He told me it was probably just a harmless garter snake and to use the small net to in the shed to scoop it out and toss it into the woods. Since he was watching me, I walked straight to the pool shed and then pretended I was a Nobel-award winning herpetologist. This enabled me to stifle my urge to scream, wrap the net around the specimen, then hurl it as far as I could. It landed about three feet away, tangled in a low bush. It's fine, I thought, someone else can deal with it now.

Alex also wisely insisted that I had to re-learn how to drive a car. Although most teenagers count the days until they get their learner's permit at sixteen, I'd grown up in Manhattan, where a monthly garage fee was the same price as the rent on a studio apartment. There was no reason to drive, anyway. I walked, took public transportation or cabs everywhere.

I had finally earned my driver's license at age twenty-one when I returned from college, mainly because I needed it as an ID. I didn't drive again until I married Alex, who patiently re-taught me how to drive, so I could get myself to yoga class or Guido's Fresh Marketplace in Great Barrington, which made me feel right at home.

Thursday, May 27, 1999: Since we both worked long hours during the week, we looked forward to spending long weekends in the country, which meant leaving on Thursday night.

On one particular Thursday, I was at the wheel, driving through a horrible storm, with hail slamming against the windshield like bullets. Visibility was beyond poor and I was clutching the steering wheel so tightly my fingers had to be pried off when we pulled into our driveway. Soon after we arrived, our next-door neighbor, a lovely woman nicknamed Carp appeared at our door to report that, during the week, the dozen birdfeeders spread over their property had been smashed to the ground by a black bear.

"What happened?" I asked, feeling the panic rise in my chest.

"It was a momma bear with her two cubs. We caught it on our infra-red video monitor on the side of the deck."

"Ah," I commented, trying to sound as if this were just an ordinary piece of gossip that country neighbors shared as they hung their sheets out to dry on clotheslines strung between majestic oak trees. "I've read that momma bears are very dangerous when their cubs are in tow, and will do anything to protect them," I added. "Have you seen them since you're back?"

"Yes," she responded, "we saw them this morning near your swimming pool." Just lucky it was too cold for a dip. Alex and I noticed that our birdhouse was down, too. I guess the ball of sunflower seeds inside was like M&Ms to bears. The sighting of the momma bear was much more disturbing than that of a herd of lazy deer. I immediately emailed my best friend from childhood, Brook. Her words of comfort were:

"You may want to rent *Legends of the Fall* which will dispute any possible claims that bears are vegetarians. (Daughter) Brett, who lived all too intimately with them in Bozeman, had a neighbor whose dog became a bear tapas. I never felt secure roaming their acreage ringing sleigh bells and carrying pepper spray — the accepted bear repellents. Why should I carry a condiment to make myself more palatable? If pepper spray, why not French sea salt? They find bells in bears' bellies..."

Later that afternoon, I wandered over to Carp and David's house to view the tape. Over cocktails, my nature-loving neighbor then admitted that she might have been partially at fault. Two nights ago, she had put some raw chicken out for the crows in the birdhouses. "Thoughtful of you," I responded, and couldn't help asking, "So what's next? A salt lick for the deer? Carrion for the vultures?"

This same nature lover reassured me, however, that she takes her shotgun with her when she walks her ancient Labrador retriever at night, because of the coyotes and mountain lions.

(It was the first I had heard of the presence of these two species in the neighborhood. Was there any question that I would sell the house immediately after Alex died?) But I couldn't help loving Carp, despite her eccentricities. She has a great sense of humor, was once a professional 'nose', and shares her rare Hen-of-the-Woods mushrooms with me, a limited number of which spring up under their enormous oak tree every year.

Since one of the main reasons we had a house in the country was so that Alex could have his garden, our next step was to purchase fifty pounds of soil and mulch. Once the soil had been delivered and spread over the garden area, we headed for Ward's, the local overpriced nursery, to purchase dozens of flats of young vegetables. As we drove home, I was excited and terrified. Just think, this summer, Ms. Robbins will be appearing in the role of The Farmer!

I had a great time at the nursery, wandering around and looking at all the sprouts and the seed packages affixed to them with photos of what the mature vegetables would look like. I felt as if I were reading the ingredients in a cookbook, or on a menu. I couldn't wait to watch them grow and then serve them to my family in inspired new recipes. We bought three kinds of tomatoes, two kinds of lettuce, broccoli, peas, zucchini, sugar snaps, and pumpkins as well as the obligatory herbs — basil, mint, oregano, chives, and rosemary. I felt myself channeling Martha Stewart, thinking about how I was going to carve pumpkins in an elaborate Victorian lace pattern in the fall to decorate our front door.

The initial planting, however, was going to have to be a solo act, since Alex was busy dealing with a tree surgeon, an exterminator, a carpenter, and a painter. Since the house hadn't been lived in for several months, there was a lot of work that had to be done.

Even though I was a city kid, I had grown up watching my mother plant and water and weed everything from pansies, geraniums, and berries to pine trees and weeping willows on our penthouse terrace. Since it was seventeen floors above the sidewalk, however, the garden was free of any fauna save the occasional disoriented squirrel, who had climbed the side of the building, plus the usual flock of filthy pigeons. I never got involved in her gardening efforts, refusing even to water, much less transplant the dozens of flats of annuals that arrived every spring.

So the physical act of planting was brand new to me. It was hard work, and even though I *thought* I knew what I was doing, once I was actually kneeling in the earth, yanking the vulnerable-looking plants out of their plastic pots, I was sure I was doing everything wrong — planting them upside down, burning them with too much fertilizer, drowning them with too much water. Kneeling on the ground was difficult, the gloves I had bought at the nursery were too big, plus there were bugs everywhere. When I'd try to swat them, I mostly succeeded in smearing dirt on my forehead and cheeks. By noon, I'd gotten a Charley horse and could barely move my right elbow, shoulder, and wrist.

We had to do another run to Ward's late that afternoon for more soil. That's when I made another discovery: If the deer and other Rodentia didn't get my vegetable sprouts during the week, the frost would. I gleaned this from our salesman, who casually mentioned that it was a little early to be slamming things into the ground. As the color drained from my face, he reassured me that all I had to do was run outside and "cover the beds." Cover them with *what?* Shower curtains? An old camp blanket? A Persian rug? I made a mental note to add the *Farmer's Almanac* to my required reading list.

But at least it had stopped raining, the cluster flies and ladybugs in the living room had pretty much died out, and the ant population was *almost* under control, thanks to the pesticide people. Unfortunately, I was not prepared for the stream of carpenter ants that tumbled out of the sugar bowl and into my steaming cup of tea. I shrieked and dropped the sugar bowl onto the stove, where the sugar seared black bubbles into the brand-new ceramic top, still hot from the boiling teakettle. I'd been wary of buying an electric cooktop and now, my suspicions were confirmed. Still, I liked the smell of caramel in the air.

I left a pile of Cerama Bryte on the flat glass burner overnight and scrubbed it until my arm went numb the next morning. Still, I couldn't buff out the scorch marks.

Late July: Several of the vegetables actually grew to edible size; the hardiest were the tomatoes, zucchini, and pumpkins. But Ariel and I were most impressed by the gorgeous crop of broccoli! It was a vibrant bright green, with large stalks and beautiful full florets. We brought in three stalks and left them on the kitchen counter, thrilled to think that we were at last part of the farm-to-table movement. Maybe I *was* cut out for country life, after all. I was thinking of inviting Carp and David over for dinner to sample the first of summer's bounty.

A few minutes after Ariel put them on the counter, I looked down at them, and rubbed my eyes. The bright green stalks seemed to be making their way toward the sink. "Funny," I said to Ariel, "They almost seem to be alive!"

She picked one up, regarded it closely, then dropped it like a hot potato and screamed so loud I thought the glass window panes would shatter. I looked closely and had to stifle one of my own screams. Hundreds of bright green aphids, camouflaged in the exact green of the broccoli, swarmed all over the stalks and florets.

She put on rubber gloves and gingerly picked them up, keeping them at arm's length, and brought them outside to a trash can, replicating the same technique as me with the garden snake. Aha, I thought, the apple doesn't fall far from the urban tree.

I wondered if it were too late to make a run to the supermarket.

August 1999

Random Act of Kindness

AS PART OF A surgery prep, I had to have MRIs on two consecutive days: brain on Tuesday, spinal on Wednesday. Overseeing the procedure on both days was a slightly gruff middle-aged Ukrainian technician. As he looked over my chart on Tuesday, Konstantin's eyebrows shot up. "Happy Birthday, one day early," he said in his pronounced Russian accent.

"Thank you," I replied, surprised and touched.

The next morning, he wished me an even more enthusiastic "Happy Birthday," before sliding me inside the machine. At the end of the procedure, when I got up from the table, he drew a bouquet of pale pink roses edged in red from behind his back, adding, "For you."

I had been holding it together pretty well since hearing the new diagnosis, but kicking off my birthday wedged inside an MRI machine for an hour would not have been my first choice. So, at the sight of those roses, my eyes welled with tears. The gesture transformed a stressful medical procedure into an experience of pure joy. I'd found myself on the receiving end of an unexpected act of kindness and, with that, Wednesday became one of the best birthdays ever.

submitted to the New York Times "Metropolitan Diary"
November 14, 2018

"For women, as well as for men, identity is largely cultivated through a sense of personal achievement, primarily through a career."

~ *Betty Friedan*

V

A Career in Wine and Food

My partner, Brian Dunn, and I co-founded the
Dunn-Robbins Group, where I remained for twenty-three years.

The Campari Door Closes

PART I: FOR ALMOST ten years, I served as the Director of Communications for Campari USA, the American company that oversaw the importing, distribution, and marketing of the famous Italian aperitif. Every quarter, our company would hold depletion report meetings in the conference room of the U.S. headquarters, located in The Delmonico, a modern office building on 59th Street off Madison Avenue in New York City.

The Campari USA offices were spread over the entire twelfth floor. The conference room contained a custom-made table of highly polished wood and surrounded with cushioned leather chairs. At one end of the room, a large mirrored bar area was framed by shelves artfully filled with Campari-logoed cocktail glasses and mixers. A second custom-made mahogany bar extended the width of the conference room and served as its focal point. At the far end stood the *pièce de resistance*, a four-foot tall shiny brass espresso machine with a free-standing brass eagle perched on top.

The particular depletion report forever burned in my memory took place on July 20, 1994. The participants included the main employees of Campari USA: The President, the CEO, the CFO, the Director of Communications (me), the Director of Marketing (Steve), the Logistics Manager, twelve regional Sales Managers from across the county and, most importantly, from their Milan headquarters, Signor Marco Perelli-Cippo, Campari's Export Director.

By 8:50 a.m., we were all in our seats around the conference table, ready for the meeting. A four-inch stack of depletion reports detailing the number of cases sold in each major region across the U.S. was placed directly in front of each of us. The reports broke down Campari sales by city and state in a mind-numbing collection of numbers and statistics. Reviewing them would take most of the day.

We all knew, going into that meeting, that our numbers were bad. Despite expensive advertising and marketing campaigns, sales were not just flat — they were declining. Campari was a hard sell in America. Every restaurant and bar in most major cities had the requisite single bottle on the bar, in plain view. But more often than not, it had been there for years, and was three-quarters full, so the beverage director was in no hurry to replace it. Americans, having been weaned on Coca-Cola, have a sweet tooth and Campari has a uniquely bitter, herbal taste. This high-proof spirit comes as even more of a shock to the American palate because its beautiful deep red color sets up the expectation of a sweet flavor. But with the first sip, all fantasies of strawberry or raspberries are blown away. Many Americans say Campari tastes like cough syrup.

The company worked valiantly to counteract this image. One campaign touted the Negroni, which had a brief run as the chic cocktail of the 1950s and again in the 1970s at gay bars, where it was considered worldly and sophisticated. Another campaign addressed the problem in a rather risqué manner by coyly asking celebrities about *Their First Time* (the first time they tasted Campari, of course). But nothing seemed to work. The American consumer didn't like the taste and, worse, wasn't interested in *acquiring* the taste. Nor could they have cared less that Campari was wildly popular throughout Italy, where it was consumed under iconic Campari-logoed patio umbrellas with matching ashtrays. So ubiquitous, the drink was considered Italy's Coca-Cola.

Given the exorbitant rent of our Madison Avenue floor-through office with its custom-designed furniture along with the salaries and benefits of about twenty full-time employees, the thought had not escaped all of us sitting around that table that Campari USA was hemorrhaging money. We knew we were in for a tough day with Signor Perelli-Cippo, but were totally unprepared for his opening remarks when he walked into the conference room at 9:00 o'clock sharp, dressed, as always, in an impeccably tailored black suit, light blue shirt, and silk Ferragamo tie. His black hair was cut very short, in a style that Americans would consider a Marine buzz cut.

I don't remember him bothering to say, "Good morning." But I do remember him saying, "Okay everyone, put your office keys on the table. You're all fired. You need to empty out your desks and vacate the premises by five o'clock."

A low buzz moved around the table as we all tried to take in this news. Some people got up silently and left the room, walking like robots. In front of each empty chair, the four-inch piles of depletion reports remained untouched.

The Marketing Director and I looked at each other with shock and disbelief. "Aileen, pinch me," Steve said. "Tell me I didn't hear what I just heard."

I pinched him and said, "Okay, I pinched you, but now I still have to tell you that I heard exactly what you just heard."

I walked across the hall, numb. I had worked at Campari USA for almost a decade. I had my own office, with a window facing east that opened onto a breathtaking cityscape. I had my own furniture, my own computer, a separate phone extension, my own file cabinets. This was more than just a job and a salary. I took pride in my work and being Director of Communications was part of my identity. I was a respected member of the team, even though I was a woman in the male-dominated world of wine and spirits. I really liked the people I worked with, and despite every indication that Campari Aperitivo was a very hard sell to Americans, I personally loved it, and had had great hopes for it.

I started opening my file cabinets — in those days, people kept hard copies of documents — but had trouble focusing on the files and their contents. I had Signor Perelli-Cippo's ruthless words running through my head. Many of us had worked there for a decade or more. Now he was letting us go, unceremoniously, without even a brief acknowledgment, like "First, I'd like to thank you all for your years of service…" something, anything, to soften the blow. But no.

I had until 5:00 p.m. to clear out my office.

Someone must have called the building super because, within an hour, giant dumpsters were wheeled into the hallway. Throughout the day, I made countless trips to toss armloads of manila files and their contents into the large metal containers. When I pulled open my first file drawer, I thought it would be difficult to pore over ten years' worth of work to decide what to toss and what to take. There were speeches, presentations, ad copy, brochures and tasting notes, press releases and the resulting articles, field-training manuals, notes from national sales seminars, plans and reports on promotional events.

But it had all turned from gold to straw and I saw no reason to keep it. I made a few exceptions: the beautiful four-color brochures; reproductions of early Campari posters, and some photos from a few of the events I had produced. There were shots of me with Milton Glaser and Sirio Maccioni, and a shot of the whole team visiting Campari's HQ outside Milan. And I couldn't resist a few photos from one of my favorite events, the party at a downtown club with featured guests Andy Warhol and Kelly LeBrock. The model-turned-star of *The Woman in Red,* LeBrock was slated to shoot a television commercial for Campari in Milan in the coming fall, and the promotion was slated to begin in New York.

The morning of our event, the manager of the Valentino boutique brought over several ensembles in her model size four, carefully selected for the range of events focused on her, which went from early morning through late night. But unbeknownst to everyone, Kelly was five-months pregnant (this was clear to me when I entered her hotel room at 8:00 a.m. and found her tucking into waffles and eggs and bacon, washed down with a strawberry milkshake). The entire wardrobe had to be returned to the store and exchanged for several sizes larger. Naturally, the cocktail spokesmodel declined all alcoholic beverages throughout the day and night.

I limited myself to what I could carry home with my two arms. Although I was shocked and terrified at losing my job, there was also something liberating about purging ten years of documents. With it, came the idea that I could try something new. It took several days before I could even talk about the mass firing, even with friends and family. But once the numbness wore off, I started to relish the thought of a new career.

PART II: I hadn't taken a real vacation in about five years so, before I started job hunting I decided to head to Aspen. There, I would spend a few weeks with old and dear friends at the Aspen Music Festival, where I had studied and performed for three summers. But two days after the ignominious firing, I started feeling nervous about being unemployed, so I called my friend Steve, a Senior VP at the *Wine Spectator*, and asked if he knew of any people I should call when I returned from Aspen. "Yes," he said, without missing a beat. "You gotta call Brian Dunn. He knows everyone in the business. And don't think of it as an interview — it's just networking."

I hung up with Steve and called Brian who said, sure, he'd meet me, how was tomorrow? His office was at one of the country's largest ad agencies, TBWA, which handled huge national accounts such as the Energizer Bunny, Absolut Vodka, and Evian.

The following day, I got dressed in a navy silk suit, an Hermes scarf and high heels. I showed up a little early, but as soon as Brian saw me, he beckoned me into his office. He was smart and quick, with a good sense of humor and we chatted easily. He told me about the Wines from Spain account at TBWA, which sounded interesting, but I wasn't really paying much attention, since I thought this was just a social call, and hadn't even brought a resumé.

After about an hour, Brian turned to me and said, "OK, when can you start?"

"When can I start *what*?" I asked.

"Start working as the Senior Account Executive for Wines from Spain."

"Ah. The Wines from Spain account. Ah." I was stalling for time. "Well, I'm going to Aspen for a much-needed vacation, but I'll be back in two weeks. I could start after that but, first, I need a lot more information about what this position would entail."

"Hmm," he said, "I can't wait two weeks. I need you to start immediately."

"Well, I can't start immediately," I said a little belligerently. "I have commitments I've made to several friends there, such as Murry's son's bar mitzvah."

We argued for about ten minutes, neither of us willing to budge. Eventually, however, I realized that Brian had made a strong and flattering case for why I would be perfect for the job. He also offered quite a reasonable salary without much negotiation on my part, so I caved, and said, "Okay, I'll start in one week, not two."

Although I certainly didn't admit it to him, over the past ten years I'd never taken a vacation longer than a single week and I was a little worried I might get antsy by day eight.

Brian and I started working together in August of 1994. He possessed a terrific knowledge of the industry, had lots of contacts, excellent negotiating and administrative skills, and an ability to cut to the chase, something he soon told me I could improve on. Although we didn't always agree, Brian respected my ability to present a counter-argument and our clients enjoyed the heated dialog that often erupted between us in meetings.

Four months later, in December, TBWA told us they wanted to fire our client. Wines from Spain was under the aegis of the Commercial Office of Spain, a beehive of bureaucracy funded by the Spanish Government. All of the agency's invoices had to be remitted in triplicate and, after being scrupulously analyzed and justified, would remain unpaid for sixty to ninety days. The ad agency had neither patience nor interest in maintaining the relationship. At barely a million dollars, the account was small potatoes. The agency asked us if we wanted to take on the client independently.

At this, Brian turned to me with an idea, "I say we take Wines from Spain and start our own company, as equal partners."

"Sounds good to me," I replied without missing a beat, although I had no idea what starting or co-running a company would entail.

We called Wines from Spain and told them we had some great news for them. We had just broken off from TBWA and started our own company with them as our only client, so their account would receive our full time and attention. They were thrilled.

By the end of the month, we'd launched The Dunn-Robbins Group, a strategic planning and marketing company. Over the next few years, we won several big accounts including Wines of Portugal, Wines of Argentina, and Wines of South Africa. We'd created a niche, planning and executing multi-faceted wine campaigns for entire countries. We hired representatives in five other cities and by 1998, we had ten employees.

Much to my dismay, Brian announced that he was retiring, in 2010. He was still young, quick, and creative so this news came as a shock to me. I loved the work, so I continued to run the company by myself until 2017. A twenty-three-year run.

One door closes and another door opens. I was pleased to find it was more than a cliché.

Robbins Rules of Order

These were written originally for new hires of The Dunn-Robbins Group, part of our company manual, but became more general over time.

Develop a Firm Handshake

Unless you are in China or Japan, where a weak grip from a woman is culturally acceptable, your grip should be strong. No boneless chicken or just touching the tips of the digits. Your handshake is an integral part of creating a strong first impression. When you reach for the other person's hand, make eye contact. And make sure that your hand's web (where the thumb meets the forefinger) fits snugly into the other person's web. Palm should touch palm. I have made instant hiring decisions based on a candidate's handshake.

Make Eye Contact

Look people in the eyes when you are talking to them to immediately establish a connection. Make them feel that they are the most important person in the world, and that you are hanging on their every word.

Know When to be Silent

Ask lots of interesting questions based on what you have learned about the person's life. Be a good listener; don't interrupt or start a new question before they've finished answering the previous one.

Write Thank You Notes

Always write a thank you note. Ideally, you should write it within twenty-four hours of the interview/event/gift/favor. A hand-written note is ideal, but very few people expect it any more and an email will suffice. But even though they will not be disappointed if they don't receive a hand-written note, they will be thrilled if they do receive one. It is a gesture that will be long and favorably remembered.

Stay in Touch: The Robbins Clipping Service

Think about what your friends and associates find interesting, and when you read a pertinent article, hear about a movie, blog, or podcast, send them the information.

Constantly Expand Your Horizons

Always seek new experiences. Find interesting places to go, including new restaurants, new performances, new museum exhibits. Take classes, sign up for a lecture series (my favorite is *The New Yorker Fall Festival*). Read new authors. Find new websites and blogs. Take up an instrument (the one you foolishly quit when you were young). Make yourself buy one new ingredient on most of your shopping trips. Go to different grocery stores/ markets. Try new recipes.

Life-Saving Humor

Develop and employ a sense of humor in every form of communication, especially in person. It is the best way to retain one's sanity, and it is quite disarming. Hard to dislike someone who can make you laugh.

Speak No Evil

You can make a few exceptions, among your very closest friends, but only in person, never in writing. Never speak ill of people in your own industry, since it will inevitably get back to them.

Write No Evil

Try never to write anything negative about anyone. This includes indirect comments, which requires that you double-check to whom you are forwarding an email, making sure it's an individual, not a group, and that there are no nasty bits somewhere on the string. And sending out a subsequent email stating, "Ignore previous email" just makes the recipient much more curious and far more likely to read the original email.

When Not to Call

Not that most people use the phone these days, so this rule might seem a bit antiquated, but this can still be important. Never call anyone at dinner time. Never call anyone before 9:00 a.m. or after 9:00 p.m., since early or late calls always make people think that a family member has died. And never call someone either in, or just returned from, the hospital.

Reciprocate the Invite

When someone has entertained you, either at a restaurant or at home, invite them back. Unless, of course, that is a relationship which you could happily live without, in which case the lack of reciprocation should be taken as a lack of interest. Unfortunately, few people interpret your lack of reciprocation correctly.

House Gift

a. Dinner: Flowers can be difficult, since the hostess has to stop her last-minute preparations and hunt madly for a vase, fill it with water, and arrange the flowers that you probably picked up at the Korean deli across the street. If you know the person really loves flowers, send an arrangement, which should arrive way in advance of the dinner. Alternatively, ask what the dinner is, and bring an appropriate wine.

b. Weekend: When someone invites you away for a weekend, if you can't afford an expensive house gift or your host has two of everything, bring a camera (the one on your phone will do) and take photos of the weekend activities, the people, the house, the setting, the meals. Within one or two days of returning home, print out the best shots, arrange them in an attractive album and mail it to them.

Guest = Helper

Always volunteer to help cook, serve or clean up when at someone else's house for a meal. This applies to your children; the parents of the child she or he visits will be impressed beyond words. When they comment on what a great help your child was, don't admit that such behavior never happens at home.

Other People's Kids

Pay attention to people's kids. Engage them in conversation which is interesting to them. They are often more interesting than the grown-ups.

Food Diary

Make notes of what people's most favorite and least favorite foods are. If you eat out with them frequently, you should know what they will order, both to drink and to eat, for each course. You can surprise them and order something for them if they are away from the table when the waiter comes to take their order.

"Leave 'em Wanting"

Words of wisdom passed on to me by Conrad Thibault, my first voice teacher. At the time, he was referring to creating a program for a vocal recital, but this applies to many other social situations: Leave before people get tired, or run out of subjects to talk about. In person, on the phone or on email. Corollary: Keep emails and voice mail messages as short as possible.

Treat Everyone Well

Be polite, courteous, and engaging to as many appropriate people as possible, especially people in the service business. This includes doormen and delivery men; sales help, domestic help, restaurateurs, sommeliers, and waiters; receptionists, nurses, and medical technicians. But don't spend too much time talking to waitstaff, since it is rude to your dinner guests.

Returns

Never be afraid to return or exchange items you have purchased or received as gifts. But try to stay within the acceptable period of time stated on the receipt unless you have advanced negotiating and acting skills.

Bad Taxi Behavior

Don't yell at cab drivers, especially when they are stuck in traffic and can't do anything about it. Loudly cursing will not make the gridlock disappear. The only time it is permissible to raise your voice is when you are trying to communicate your destination and the driver can't hear you because he's so busy chatting away on his cell in an incomprehensible language.

Re-invent Yourself Every Decade

This applies to your career as well as your hairstyle, make-up, treatment line, and wardrobe. What you wore when you were twenty is not appropriate when you're forty. The Alice in Wonderland hairdo with the thin headband should be updated. Start wearing hats. Learn how to wear scarves.

Focus on Who Plays a Meaningful Role in Your Life

Especially as you get older, spend your time with a few very dear friends. Life is too short to spend time with people whom you don't find interesting, who don't make you laugh and cry, or you can't make laugh and cry.

Corollary: At some point, stop making small talk.

July 2010

Speech: Women in Food Service

HELLO, MY NAME IS Aileen Robbins and I'm a restaurant junkie. Which means that I get an absolute rush every time I hear about an exciting new restaurant that is about to open and I try to get there within the first few weeks. Finding a great new place to eat is like finding a new best friend — I feel stimulated, happy, relaxed, and challenged all at the same time.

As you heard from my rather bizarre bio (*thank you, Harriet*), I have always been involved with food. Even when I was a professional opera singer, I helped support myself by writing about restaurants, foods, wines. One of the first remarks people would make, especially men, when they learned I was an opera singer, was: "Oh, you can't possibly be an opera singer, you're so *small.*" Considering they were staring directly at my chest, I knew they didn't mean they were surprised that I was 5'4" and weighed 110 lbs; what really surprised them was how flat-chested I was. My snappy retort was always, "Isn't it amazing? They just discovered that you don't store oxygen in your tits!"

My professional career in food began while I was still performing opera. For two years I worked with an excellent teacher and Chinese cook, Karen Lee, and in 1980, our book containing her recipes and my edits of her descriptions was published and nominated for a James Beard Award. I also was writing columns in newspapers and magazines: I had a byline on "Trends" in *The New York Post*, and free-lanced articles for everything from *Mademoiselle* to *Lear's*.

In 1980, I went to work for Mitchell-Manning Associates, a high-end PR firm, and had some wonderful clients, including restaurants ranging from Jim McMullen's to Le Chantilly, and products that ranged from Piper Sonoma to Neuchatel chocolates. I became Account Supervisor on Campari in 1983, and within a year Campari USA hired me away to work in-house as their Director of Communications, both on the famous Italian Aperitivo, and a few years later, on *Pampero Anniversario* (an aged rum) and a range of vodkas.

It was a rough transition to the spirits world. I showed up at my first distributor meeting out in Queens, totally inappropriately dressed in an elegant black silk suit with pearls and black pumps. There wasn't another person in the room with natural fibers touching their body and everyone's name seemed to end in a vowel. Plus, I was the only female in the room, so I would have stuck out even if I weren't ridiculously attired. About five minutes into my scrupulously well rehearsed and brilliantly organized presentation about marketing objectives for the quarter, I noticed that the men in the back row were playing cards. Trying quickly to adjust to this different environment, I yelled out, "Hey Vinnie, who's winning?"

Begrudgingly, I began to win their respect over the years, even though, as most old-timers will tell you, "the liquor business ain't no place for a lady." I spent the next decade fine-tuning the art of protective camouflage, and could tell or hear any type of joke without blushing. I thought I had made incredible headway, and was feeling quite confident over the past year, especially when I was asked to speak at an international marketing conference and the audience actually paid attention. Although I kind of missed the poker players in the back row.

But there has been some recidivism. This past June, my partner Brian Dunn and I went up to the Wine & Spirits Wholesalers Association in Boston for the most important industry event of the year. We had just incorporated and I was feeling very empowered by The Dunn-Robbins logo on my business card as well as on the door to our new offices in the Flatiron District, overlooking Madison Square Park. My partner has been in the business for over twenty years, and is well known and well respected so, at this annual convention, we kept bumping into men he knew. We had on our boldly printed name tags, but nonetheless, in more cases than I would care to admit, even though Brian would say, "let me introduce you to my *partner*, Aileen Robbins," most men would punch him in the shoulder and say, "Oh! So this is the little woman!" After the third time, he just gave up and said, "yes."

I want to thank Harriet Lembeck, who asked me to speak today. She is one of the women I respect most in the industry. Several years ago, I took her excellent wine course. Unfortunately, I entered in the middle of the semester — the first few months were on white wine, and the last were on reds. I entered on the transitional day, when she was about to launch into the study of reds, but not until the class had been given a little pop quiz. It was a quasi-blind tasting of several white wines from the first half of the semester.

I totally panicked, even though there were only eight wines and the bottles were actually lined up on the table in the front of the room, although in random order. I leaned over to Harriet and said in a hoarse, anxious voice,

"I can't possibly be expected to take this quiz — I wasn't here for the first half of the course!"

"It doesn't matter, " she said reassuringly, "it's just for fun, to see how much you know."

"This is not my idea of fun; being unprepared for a test is a recurring nightmare. I will only take a test if I can score a ninety or above."

Considering she didn't want to waste any more time discussing my compulsive overachieving personality, I was permitted to not hand in my test. What a good sport, what a sensitive soul! She is one of my favorite ladies — in or out of the wine business.

I took the second half of the course, studied hard, and passed the blind-tasting pop quiz on red wines with flying colors. That's the beauty of being in the wine and spirits industry; you are constantly learning, since every year there are new vintages, new wine regions, new spirits. You get to travel to beautiful wine regions, eat wonderful local meals complemented with local wines, and develop great friendships.

After a few years, it became abundantly clear to all of our current and prospective clients that Brian and I were equal partners. No-one ever referred to me as "the little woman" again.

Monday, July 10,1998

Event Report: Wine and EVOO Tasting

WHEN I OPENED MY eyes and looked outside the window at 6:30 a.m. on February 8th, I gasped. It was snowing. I immediately checked the weather on my phone; heavy snow predicted all day long. This was the day I was producing a very important tasting and seminars on some high-quality Italian wines and Italian Extra-Virgin Olive Oils, accompanied by the launch of two much heralded Guides, one for this year's wines, the other for its olive oils. Both the authors and many of the top producers would be present.

The events were taking place on two different floors of the Yale Club: The Grand Ballroom on the top floor, with beautiful floor to ceiling windows, and the Trumbull Room, set up for the press conference and seminars.

I got to the Yale Club at around 8:00, and by 9:30 it was snowing quite hard, all too visible from the massive French windows on three sides of the Grand Ballroom. New York wine and food tastings, especially for press and trade, which is what all of my clients focused on, were far too common. Even if the products were spectacular, and there were celebrity speakers, the competition was so fierce that only a small number of press showed up under the best of circumstances. The really top epicurean writers refuse to attend almost all large walk-around tastings; they prefer to have the winemaker visit them in their office or host them at a one-on-one lunch or dinner.

Added to that was the unwritten law of NYC RSVPs: if your guest wasn't paying for the ticket, you'd be hit with about one-third no-shows. My client had wanted — no, was *expecting* — around 400 guests, and even though I had sent out multiple creative invitations and reminders and had my staff make personal calls to over a hundred people, we still had only 250 RSVPs. The one-third ratio would be even lower if there were inclement weather and all I had to do was glance quickly at the snowflakes swirling around the windows to know that this snowstorm would serve as a real deterrent.

By this time in my career, I had been producing events — from four to 1,200 people — for twenty-two years. The vast majority of them were successful, but I always had that moment of complete animal panic when I arrived at the venue on the morning of the event and thought, no-one will show up, this will be a huge failure, my client will not pay me, and I will never work in this town again. Thoughts of locking myself in the bathroom or escaping to the nearest movie house ran on a constant tape-loop through my anxiety-riddled brain.

The load-in was a logistical and physical nightmare. There were fifty-six wine producers with a minimum of three wines each, and twenty-four olive oil producers, with three to six different olive oils each. This meant we had to move literally hundreds of cases to the eighty different stations on the perimeter and in a rectangle in the center of the room. The client had her own assistant there to help set up the room. When the assistant wasn't shrieking at me and two of my staff who also were there at 8 a.m., she and her husband were chasing after their one-year-old-son, who was crawling around on the floor among the cases of wine all morning, strewing dozens of brightly colored plastic blocks in his wake.

The assistant, from Italy, had rented the glassware, which looked like Libby's — ugly, stumpy wineglasses with a thick stem and a restaurant lip, which is a slighter thicker band around the rim of the glass. We had set up two tables in the foyer in front of the elevators, designating one table for check-in and the other for the glasses. After checking the attendees in, the charming young ladies at the check-in table (I always hired actresses as greeters) instructed guests to pick up their glass from the neighboring table. So, the first order of the day was to take the 600 heavy squat glasses out of their heavy square plastic rental crates and arrange them on the six-foot table in the hallway.

A few minutes after I finished, however, the assistant came up to me and said that she didn't want the glasses that close to the elevators; she was sure that people would bump into them with their coats and bags. Well, first of all, there was plenty of space, it's not like people were wearing raccoon coats, and anyway, they could check them downstairs; but second of all, you could have dropped these glasses off the Ballroom's balcony and they wouldn't have broken when they hit 44th Street.

So I then had to move all the glasses back into their crates, and re-set them on the table, which had been moved *inside* the room.

The Yale catering waitstaff set up the tables and table cloths, but we were responsible for putting out ice tubs, ice buckets, table signs, hashtag signs, napkins, water pitchers, baskets with bread and crackers, and wastebaskets. Then we had to move the wines and olive oils in front of the appropriate table and open the cases.

The author of the new Annual Wine Guide delivered his PowerPoint presentation in English, a PowerPoint in name only, there were no bullet points, no illustrations, just entire paragraphs lifted whole from the introduction to his book and slapped onto a mind-numbing progression of slides. He spoke good English, but the talk was long and complicated. Then the head of the olive oil consortium got up. Since he does not speak English, he had a translator, who was incomprehensible (I didn't hire her). About ten minutes into it, I started checking my cellphone for nearby movie theatres.

I then took the elevator back up to the twentieth floor, filled with dread at seeing the Grand Ballroom. The first walk-around tasting was supposed to have started half an hour ago, and I feared the room would be peopled only by the producers standing behind their tables. I literally averted my eyes when the elevator door opened. *Don't panic,* I told myself, *you can just stay in the elevator and take it back down to the ground floor*. But an unexpected sight made me gasp. Talk about miracles. The ballroom was *mobbed.* There were at least 150 attendees in front of all the tables. I thought the door had opened on the wrong floor.

The flow of new members of press and trade continued

for the next two hours and the room crackled with energy and excitement. At 3:00 p.m., the Olive Oil Seminar was scheduled for the Trumbull Room, plenty of time after the Press Conference ended for the staff to set up the room for the tasting seminar. The tables and chairs were in place. All we had to do was put down the tasting mats and brochures and pour the olive oil for a maximum seventy-two attendees.

Pouring the olive oil samples was far more difficult than it sounds. There were six teeny plastic cups on small corresponding circles on each tasting mat, the kind they put your pills in when you're in the hospital, and we had to pour one-eighth inch of olive oil into each of these mini receptacles; *that's 456 pours*. With my seriously impaired vision, I sure as hell wasn't going to try to pour olive oil from large heavy glass bottles into teeny little cups.

We had three people pouring, one of whom was the head of the Olive Oil Consortium, who was furious that there were not more people to help, but no-one was available. The waiters were helping in the Ballroom and my staff was busy with the continuous demands of a well-managed tasting — checking people in, clearing dirty plates, replenishing glassware, and assisting the producers.

Pouring the olive took a lot of time, so the tasting started more than half an hour late. This time, however, I not only had a full house — I had a waiting list! People were genuinely interested in the subject. The seminar consisted of another PowerPoint with huge chunks of text, no graphics. There was fascinating information in the presentation, but most of it was highly technical and the audience felt overwhelmed.

They snapped to attention, however, when a hard news

journalist from Reuters asked a politically-charged question about where the funding came from, both to aid the producers and produce the books. This was a reference to the recent *Agro Mafia* segment aired on *60 Minutes*, which reported on the Extra Virgin olive oil scandal. According to the report, much of the olive oil being identified as EVOO was, in fact, a mix of olive oils, all inferior, some not even from Italy. As the CBS synopsis read, *"In Italy, Bill Whitaker finds out that the long arms of the Mafia extend to agricultural products, especially olive oil, on which the mob makes huge profits by exporting imitations."*

The speaker was evasive in his response. But by then, we had run over the allotted time and I had to signal him to conclude his remarks. I was jumping up and down in the back of the room, in full view of the speaker and his translator, frantically tapping my watch and making a dramatic slicing motion in front of my throat. I then raced out of the room and over to the staircase. It was only two flights back up to the ballroom but I began feeling dizzy after the first flight. I had had nothing to eat or drink all day except a small container of coconut water. At six-fifteen, right before the second session, I raced out to buy a protein shake across the street. Almond butter, yogurt, and hemp sounded healthy but tasted horrible. I took two sips and threw it away.

By the last session, from 6:30 to 8:30 p.m., the producers had been on their feet for about six straight hours, and the strain of making pleasantries in a foreign language had worn them down. Most had a glazed look in their eyes. They'd settled in the chairs behind their tables and were talking among themselves.

This was my favorite time, however, since I had invited

lots of friends to this last portion. The hard part was over and I could relax and enjoy the party in this elegant room. Even the snow, still falling, began to look beautiful to me. But after ten consecutive hours of non-stop work, I was running on fumes.

People drifted out at around 9:00 p.m. By 10:00 we had packed everything up. And by 11:00, I was home and too tired to eat. I couldn't fall asleep until 1:00 a.m., thinking of all the follow-up that had to be done.

Woke up at six the next morning, due to the internal alarm clock which I am incapable of shutting off, and outlined my to-do list; I had a post-mortem meeting with my client in my office at ten to evaluate what had gone well, what could have gone better. I forced myself to stay in bed until 6:30 a.m. but then got dressed and went to the gym, thinking that would get the blood flowing. Draped myself over a bike for a few minutes, but was too tired to move the pedals, so I plopped myself down on one of the soft mats to do some stretching. That lasted about two minutes; I then just lay down on my back. Felt myself slipping into a coma, so got up and took a shower. Was at my desk by 8:30 a.m., plenty of time to type up my report, including a detailed list of the attendees.

Personal Summary: about 280 people showed up, and there was positive feedback about the wines, the olive oils, and the accompanying Guides. The highlight for many was the Agro Mafia story. Some retailers and beverage directors expressed interest in the wines and olive oils, but the initial enthusiasm expressed by potential buyers at a tasting often wanes unless there is immediate follow-up on the part of the producer. Some people purchased the very comprehensive and well researched Guides.

Client Summary: My client told the producers that there were 400+ attendees. They also assured them that there were lots of important contacts made, which would generate sales.

I wondered if I should show them the accurate check-in list which my two check-in hostesses and I had spent hours compiling. Then I thought better of it; the bottom line was that my client and their producers were pleased. And the irony is that, having done a good job, the client will probably ask me to take on this event again next year. The word *no* springs immediately to mind.

February 8, 2016

VI

Oniomania:

[oh-nee-uh-mey-nee-uh, -meyn-yuh] noun

AN UNCONTROLLABLE DESIRE TO BUY THINGS.

WHOEVER SAID MONEY
CAN'T BUY HAPPINESS DIDN'T
KNOW WHERE TO SHOP.

I wish retail therapy was covered by
my health insurance.

Anonymous

Retail Therapy: Caveat Emptor

SATURDAY MARKED MY SUMMER sale shopping spree and, just this once, I might have set a compulsive shopping record. Considering the deep period of debt that I am currently struggling through, this is remarkable. I have dedicated a few sleepless nights mulling over which savings account, money market fund, or stock portfolio I will invade to cover the particular tsunami of debt that is currently crashing over me.

For the record, I'd spent several thousand dollars on home renovations this spring, prompted by my daughter, who'd started referring to apartment as "the crack den" due to some peeling paint, a few discolored kitchen tiles, and a missing fixture. Within three weeks, everything was painted, polished, scrubbed, dusted, waxed, and I'd had someone lay a new floor in my kitchen to go with the cheery bright-yellow newly painted walls. You now need sunglasses to walk from the kitchen door to the sink.

I'd also made a hefty down-payment to an electrician a month ago, although he has yet to show up. In addition to the electricity in the hallway being out, which means I need a flashlight to get anything out of my largest closet, it's also out in half my bedroom, where neither the television nor the air conditioning works. But the upside is, if I sweat while I sleep, I'll be thinner when I wake up in the morning.

Back to this weekend's purchases. Most were made on July 4th, a day when I thought I'd be safe doing a little window shopping because everything would either be closed or running fabulous holiday sales. My window-shopping trip didn't go quite as planned, so here's a small accounting:

1. Betsey Bunky Nini: I went directly to this boutique with an old store-credit in hand. When I got to the register with the navy pants and pale blue-grey shirt I'd found on sale, the salesgirl informed me my purchase total was $40 less than my $316 credit amount.

Since the credit dated from 2002, she told me kindly, if I didn't use it all that very day, I would lose it. Betsey Bunky Nini stocks very few items in the $40 range, but I ended up finding a filmy oriental-print chiffon long sundress, priced substantially higher than my remaining credit. And I was so touched by the salesgirl's willingness to honor my outdated store credit that I bought it. I have no idea when or where I will ever wear a filmy oriental-print chiffon sundress, but its bizarre cut would be appropriate at an avant-garde dance performance in Brooklyn or Paris. Chances are much higher of my attending such a performance at the latter than the former.

2. Todd's: Found a very practical navy shoulder bag and matching sandals, deeply discounted. Sandals will take some breaking in, since the straps across the toes are made out of stiff

navy patent leather. Will have to take them to the shoemaker to be stretched.

3. Bergdorf Goodman: I was in luck! Their amazing summer shoe sale was going on. Found two pairs of high-heeled sandals, one Chanel, in dark denim with silver heels, the other Gucci, beige "G's" with turquoise trim, neither of which I will be able to wear for more than forty-five seconds. I will offer the Chanel sandals to Ariel, since I now realize, they are a size too large. Not returnable, but a total steal.

4. Anne Fontaine: This French designer store on Madison does ladies' blouses only in black or white. They're beautiful, and I managed to find one that actually fit my 34A torso. The blouse has lace flower cut-outs so, naturally, the saleslady strongly recommended their white camisole to go underneath. "I can't possibly buy another white camisole," I told her, "I can barely close my lingerie drawer, as it is."

"But Madame," she replied solemnly. "There are many shades of white. Only *this* one will match the shirt exactly." She then persuaded me to purchase a special mesh bag for the delicate wash cycle. Seems you can't send their white shirts out for dry-cleaning because they will come back slightly yellow.

5. Hermès: The white suit in the window of their flagship store on Madison Avenue was heart-stoppingly beautiful. Chalk white, no collar, just an elegant long jacket with a thin strip of silk piping, in their signature orange, running the length of the jacket near the buttons. Had to go in and try it on. The fabric was cool and sensuous, like nothing I've felt before or since. The suit was lined in silk and it fit like a dream; no alterations needed;

I could have worn it out of the store. Literally brought tears to my eyes. Not on sale, but not totally unaffordable if I didn't buy anything else, including food, until Thanksgiving. So I told the sales lady that I had to think about it, since every time I wore white, I became a magnet for red wine and marinara sauce from anyone in range. So unless it came with its own dry-cleaning contract or laundress, it was too impractical. What restraint!

Then, just as I was about to leave the gorgeous wood-paneled, softly-lit dressing room on the second floor of the Hermès boutique, I had a fashion epiphany. I realized that what separated me from the suit of my dreams was neither the price nor the cleaning bills. The real issue was that *I had no place to wear this cruelly chic suit.* The problem wasn't economic; it was *social.* Had I been invited to dinner at Alain Ducasse? Lunch on a yacht? Cocktails on the roof of the new Mandarin Oriental? I checked my calendar. Nope. The only place I could wear the Hermes suit was when shopping for other expensive clothes. A life-changing revelation.

6. Ferragamo: Again, big seasonal sale. Couldn't resist a matching silk sweater set with this startling, bold bright-blue fish pattern all over it. Don't know what I was thinking. I will not even be anywhere near the sea for the rest of the year. Tried it on at home, looked like an animated fish tank.

By the time I returned home, heavily laden with shopping bags, I was exhausted. Lugged the shopping bags into my bedroom, where I tried to find room to squeeze new clothes into already-full drawers and closets. Had immediate second thoughts about a majority of the purchases, but the good and bad news is, most were on sale and not returnable. And I realized that, for the rest of my life, I will regret not buying the white Hermès suit.

I silently resolve not to shop until the first snowfall.

July 2004

Unauthorized Biography: Closet Tells All

I AM STUFFED TO overflowing. You can't shove another hanger in me. And it's not just crowded; it's noisy. Filled with incessant chatter. Every item of clothing has a story and every one of them wants to tell it — when it was bought, where it was bought, what Aileen's mood was like when she bought it, where she wore it, what was the impression she wanted to make, and what was the impression she actually *did* make.

And lemme tell you, some of these dresses and skirts and shirts and jackets may have fancy labels, but they're not very polite. I have to keep reminding them, "One at a time, one at a time." They're so narcissistic, they all think their story is the best. I've even seen a jealous YSL silk shirt nudge a Bruno Cuccinelli sweater dress off the hanger.

She's terrible at giving clothes away so, on my racks and shelves, I have biographical material dating back most of her adult life.

Here are a few of their stories.

In the back of her closet are the business suits which

survived last year's purge. After twenty-four years of running The Dunn-Robbins Group, she finally closed her office. Her partner Brian was well-respected in the wine biz, but he was no Beau Brummel. He never noticed when she wore a new outfit or dyed her hair red. The whole closet hated him for that.

I'll never forget her first major presentation for their main client, Wines from Spain. She had carefully chosen an ensemble and hung it on the closet door the night before. But when she woke up the next morning, it just didn't feel right. So, she proceeded to rifle through the entire closet, trying on one suit and blouse after another, throwing piece after piece on the bed. She spent almost an hour putting herself together that morning, finally settling on all Armani: Icy blue-grey satin shirt, light grey wool jacket, dark grey pencil skirt. Black and white thin-striped silk scarf. And big silver earrings.

She was running late, so she left my door wide open and didn't have time to hang everything back up properly. The clothes lay crumpled over every inch of the queen-sized bed and, all day long, I had to listen to their complaints. "I don't know why she bothers to buy expensive clothes if she's not willing to take proper care of us," sniffed the Chanel jacket. "She should just go to Loehman's."

We were relieved when she came home that evening and took time to hang everything up. But I could tell she wasn't happy. The silk shirt spilled the beans. Seemed that several people at the meeting had commented on how great she looked, including the Director of Wines from Spain, who happened to be a woman. But her partner Brian hadn't said a word about her outfit, not even to put her in a positive frame of mind before the presentation.

Once it was over, however, he complimented her on the presentation. The program and budget were enthusiastically approved, and the client was more than satisfied, but she was still miffed. "Get over it," I muttered, "he's your straight business partner, not your gay best friend."

We hoped she'd find a beau who appreciated her — and us. And, a few months later, a doctor, whom she'd known for many years, came into her life. They had always liked each other but he was frequently married. Now, though, he was in the process of divorcing wife number three. Boy, if that isn't a red flag. But we were willing to overlook it because he was smart and funny and he had *great* taste. To celebrate their three-month dating anniversary, he bought her an exquisite Hermes scarf, a symphony in pale greens and peach in *Les Fleurs de l'Opéra* pattern, a romantic reference. They both loved opera and, the next night, he was taking her to his family's box at the Metropolitan Opera for the first time. It would be their last night together for a week. He was taking his kids to Florida for spring break the next morning.

That night, when she returned home with his gift, she went through each hanger in turn, holding up the scarf. Nothing was quite right. Even though the rod was sagging under the weight of the accumulated garments, packed in like sardines, we all groaned at her senseless complaint, "I have nothing to wear."

The next morning, she did what any outwardly confident, inwardly insecure urban professional woman would do. She put the scarf back in its iconic square orange box, slipped it into her oversized shoulder bag, and headed to the stores. I know, I know, it sounds bizarre. Who starts with the scarf, then goes hunting for a suit to wear with it?

She started on Madison Avenue, stopping in a half-dozen boutiques. Nothing. She then moved over to Fifth. She ran through Bergdorf's and finally found herself at Saks.

There, she found an exquisite Loewe suede leather suit. Soft as butter. What made her audibly gasp and hold the saleswoman's shoulder for support, however, were its colors: Pale celadon green and creamy orange sorbet, which blended perfectly with the scarf. And, this heart-stoppingly beautiful suit *was on sale.* Which was lucky, since there was no way she could have afforded it, even if she gave up lunch for the rest of the year. The Loewe suit's heart also beat faster, sensing it was going to a good home.

Both skirt and jacket fit like a dream — also lucky, since there was no time for alterations (okay, the sleeves were a little long, but we were willing to overlook that, too). It would be perfect to wear to the opera that night.

When he picked her up, he showered her with compliments — he'd never seen her look more beautiful, the colors were so flattering, how brilliant that she had such a perfect suit to complement the scarf. The performance was Rossini's *L'Italiana in Algeri*, a marvelous frothy farce, and the costumes were in all shades of pastel. She felt at one with this sherbet-colored production and the world. The Loewe suit also had a wonderful time; it loved Rossini. The only time it flinched was when the beau slung his slightly sweaty hand over her shoulder and pressed it into the pale orange suede.

They shared a crosstown cab although they'd be staying in their respective homes that night. Along the way, he let slip that the trip to Florida would include his children from his last two marriages and — a fact he'd managed to omit —they'd be accompanied by soon-to-be-ex-wife number three. "Just to help look after all the children," he stammered.

"Uh-huh," she said, "and you'll be sharing a room with her?"

No answer. They had reached her street. She stomped out of the cab and slammed the door. She raced into her apartment, made a beeline for the bedroom, and practically ripped the poor suit off. Then, adding insult to injury, she hissed, "You can be sure I'm not wearing *you* any time soon!" The entire wardrobe gasped.

The suit spent the night doing a backbend over the handlebars of the stationary bike in the corner and didn't get hung up properly until the next morning. When everyone asked how the evening was, it shrugged its beautiful suede shoulders and sighed. We all felt terrible.

We never heard from the doctor again, who, as it turned out, was also sleeping with his nurse. But a few months later, on Aileen's fiftieth birthday, Brian surprised all of us by showing up at the office with a square flat orange box. Inside was a beautiful Hermès scarf, in her favorite color, dark blue, which goes with at least half of the residents who call my closet home.

October 2017

Magic Out of a Hat

MY FIRST JOB OUT of college at age twenty-two was as an editor at Drama Bookshop Publishers and my first assignment was to edit a major work by a celebrated director and teacher. The day before our first meeting, I panicked. How could I presume to edit the work of this distinguished man of the theatre? As a fledgling opera singer who knew about costumes, my first instinct was to dress the part, so I bought a dark green felt fedora with a feather, which I wore at a rakish angle.

Once in his office, however, I spent the first twenty minutes paralyzed about indoor hat protocol. Do I leave it on or take it off? I finally decided to leave it on. That decision got me through the first of many successful editing sessions. It also got me hooked on hats.

I was joined in my hat mania by my dearest friend, Naomi, a prima ballerina at the American Ballet Theatre. She wore floppy picture hats with large silk flowers and ribbons while I wore more tailored fedoras and cloches. We could always be sure of being seated in the front window of restaurants.

After a few years, I left the stage, joined the work force, and eventually started my own company. Sadly, I wore hats only to protect myself from snow, rain, or sun. I did, however, spend an inordinate amount of time and money trying to calm my mane of very thick, often frizzy hair.

Two years ago, after taking an immunotherapy drug to fight Stage IV melanoma, I started to lose my hair. Within a few weeks, when I realized I couldn't find a rubber band small enough for my ponytail and most of what I saw was scalp, not hair, I made an appointment at one of the wigmaker salons on Memorial Sloan Kettering's list. I chose the same hair color as my own and had it styled in my usual shoulder-length page boy. When the wig was ready and I tried it on, I was shocked to realize that I was fighting back tears. This was what I used to look like, at least on a non-humid day.

I wasn't being vain; I just didn't want to look sick and have people treat me differently. I wore the wig out of the store and had a few blissful hours. But by the end of the evening, the wig proved to be itchy, tight, and confining. If I wasn't careful, it skewed to one side. After wearing it four times, I dropped the wig onto its Styrofoam head, stabbed it with pins, put it in the back of my closet and went hat shopping.

Over the next few weeks, I visited three top milliners in New York and collaborated with them on designing hats for a wide range of occasions. I had two favorites. One was a stiff straw bowler, orange on the crown and denim blue on the brim. For a business event in Soho one Saturday afternoon, I created an outfit based around this hat: Max Mara orange jacket, a Moschino jewel-print blouse, taupe pants, orange shoulder bag, and navy suede flats. Two blocks from the event, I was stopped by the *Look Book* page team of *New York Magazine*. They asked if they could shoot some photos of me and shot dozens. Despite feeling like an imposter, I have rarely felt more glamorous.

My other favorite hat was a black velvet brimless oval fascinator, a word from the milliner's lexicon to describe an "ornamental, lightweight hat with feathers, flowers, beads, etc., worn to special events." Over the front and sides of this fascinator was a black veil sparkling with jet beads, and in the back was a large multi-looped heavy satin bow. I wore the hat tilted over the right eye. It screamed for smudgy black eye make-up and bright red lipstick. I wore it to the opera, to concerts and cocktail parties. Total strangers would come up and compliment me on it. But when I took it off, I went from the belle of the ball to the kid on chemo.

I kept the fascinator for special occasions but, for about a year and a half, I wore a hat every single day. Each offered some special magic that made me feel attractive and normal at a time when I was neither. I found a six-foot hat rack, a tall metal pole with arms sticking out in all directions to hold twenty-two hats and gave it a place of prominence in my entrance hallway.

About six months ago, my hair began to grow back. Of course, I was happy to see the regrowth but, ironically, the added volume meant that most of my custom-made hats didn't fit anymore. Even though the hats played a major role in helping get me through the past two years and the hat rack itself is a work of art, I think it's time to give most of them away. Not all of them; some I can have stretched. And yesterday I spotted a dove-grey felt Borsalino with a band of feathers which I definitely have to try on.

August 2014

VII
Sick Humor

Title courtesy of Ralph Pine,
who gave me my first job at
Drama Bookshop Publishers.
May he rest in peace.

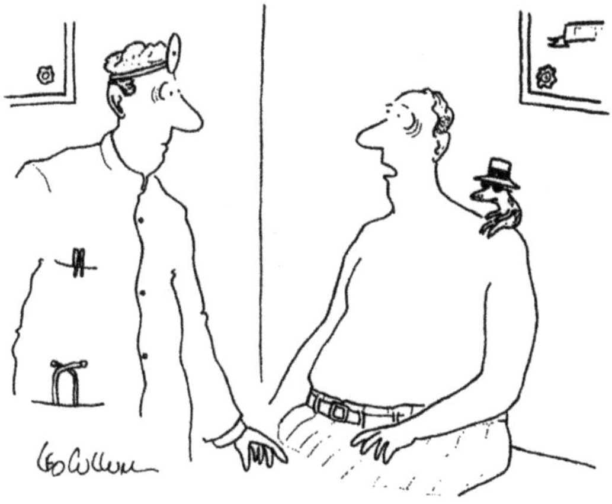

"I have a suspicious looking mole on my shoulder."

"I'll distract him with my complete medical history, and then you can make your move."

Sixty-Four Years of Perfect Health

IN THE SUMMER OF 2011, I noticed a white bump on the top of my right leg, about an inch above my knee. It looked like an insect bite, but it hadn't gone away in several weeks and, by the fall, it began to feel sensitive to the touch. I would have continued to ignore it, but it reminded me of the bump that had shown up on my daughter's collarbone many years ago. That bump had been diagnosed as Stage IV Hodgkins.

Even though I wasn't much of an alarmist, and had always been the healthy one in the family, I decided to have it checked out. So I went to my usual dermatologist, who took a look and said it was a benign cyst, nothing to worry about. I said it was bothering me and wanted to have it removed, so he gave me the name of a plastic surgeon.

I made an appointment immediately, traveling all the way uptown to Columbia Presbyterian at West 168th Street. The surgery took about fifteen minutes while I half-reclined on a paper-covered chair. He gave me a local anesthetic, made a little incision, excised the supposed fat cells, and sewed it up with four stitches. I felt totally fine, but as a little reward, went directly to Bloomingdale's, where they were having a sale on fall coats.

That was in late October. A few weeks later, I left to lead a group of wine writers on a tour of Portugal. Had a great time, felt wonderful. Forgot all about the white bump. Thanksgiving came and went but, at the very end of November, I received a phone call from the nurse at the plastic surgeon's office. "You have to come in right away," she said. "Why?" I said. "The doctor needs to speak to you." Hmmm. What could he need to speak to me about, more than a month after the initial surgery?

I went to his midtown office, this time. I had barely sat down when he said, "We have the results of the biopsy. You have Stage IV Myeloma." It was one of those moments when you have two immediate reactions: First, total disbelief. You think, they must have read someone else's slide. And then you think, maybe it's true, but it's as if you're watching a movie, and this fit, healthy-looking woman gets a diagnosis, and you think, "Hell, she sure wasn't expecting that!" And then you realize that healthy-looking woman is you.

My first question was, "Why did you wait so long to tell me?" to which the doctor replied, "I didn't want to ruin your Thanksgiving." Well, gee, that made sense; why take a chance of putting a damper on someone's holiday, even though malignant cells are metastasizing throughout her body? Let's see, turkey or treatment? Better? Worse? I guess turkey won.

The procrastinating doctor did, however, redeem himself by sending me immediately to Dr. Jedd Wolchok, the leading doctor in melanoma research at Memorial Sloan Kettering, conveniently located only a few blocks from my house. He saw me the next day and did another biopsy, thereby determining that the pathologist at Columbia *had mis-read the slides* and that the correct diagnosis was *melanoma*, not myeloma, a huge difference, not only in chance of survival, but in terms of treatment. Dr. Wolchok sent me to the Memorial Sloan Kettering melanoma specialist surgeon, who gave me a date for surgery a mere two weeks away.

Surgery went well, although since she had to get "clean outlines" around the tumor site, I ended up with a long horizontal scar requiring twenty-three stitches, two inches above my knee. I had to wear a leg brace for several weeks so I wouldn't bend the knee and pop open the stitches. But they also knew that the tumor above the knee was not the primary site. A PET scan determined that there were tumors in my abdomen, arms, and legs. The decision was made to start me on immunotherapy, the new miracle approach to melanoma treatment, the field where Dr. Wolchok has been doing ground-breaking research for over a decade.

He started me on Ipilimumab, an FDA approved drug which took me two weeks to learn how to pronounce. They had had some degree of success with it; life expectancy was increased from 6-12 months to 18-24 months. Every other week, I would have a drip infusion. At first, the tumors seemed to shrink, but then the toxicity built up — liver dysfunction, acute colitis — so they had to take me off *Ipi,* which I soon learned was what everyone called it, after I had practiced long and hard to roll the full word off my tongue. In order to get my liver enzymes back to normal and treat the colitis, they put me on large doses of Prednisone, a miracle drug which is used to reverse serious conditions, but which has side effects of its own. See "Prednisone Princess Diaries" (coming up next).

July 2011

The Prednisone Princess Diaries

FRIDAY, AUGUST 3, 2012: Take first megadose of Prednisone, 120 mg.

Friday, August 4: Wake up at 4:00 a.m. with the heartbeat of a hummingbird after having slept for two hours. Although I am usually the polar opposite of Heloise with her helpful hints, from the minute my eyes flutter open, I have this mad urge to purge. I spend the next three early-morning hours emptying out closets and bureaus and even sort through the rats' nest of cosmetics and expired drugs crammed into the cabinet under the bathroom sink.

After this culling frenzy, the sun has risen, so I take Henry the English Spaniel out for a two-mile sprint around Central Park. As usual, he spends most of the time chasing squirrels. I am so wired that I spot them before he does and have to restrain myself from running up tree trunks with him.

Drop the exhausted spaniel back home at around 8:30 a.m. and then jog the twenty blocks up to my daughter Ariel's apartment. Have breakfast with her and read five books at nano-speed to my granddaughter. Then, executing my version of *The Red Shoes*, race the forty blocks from Ariel's down to Saks, which is having a great end-of-season sale. I call ahead to warn Carmela, my salesperson friend there, that the Energizer Bunny is coming to rifle through the racks. Meet her on the ninth floor and drag armloads of outfits into a fitting room.

Hop in and out of dozens of items. Best find: Stella McCartney's blue polka dot size twenty-seven peg leg jeans. Put them on as soon as I get home, but within an hour they have cut off most of the circulation in my legs. Note to self: Wear them only to accomplish brief tasks, such as riding the elevator down to the lobby to pick up the mail.

At 1 p.m., meet two best friends, Rebecca and Claudia, at the Whitney Museum on 74th Street and Madison for lunch at their restaurant, Untitled, and a special exhibit. I can't restrain myself from cross-examining the waiter about the Cedar Roasted Salmon: is it actually cooked on a cedar plank? Is the fennel raw or braised? Are the pecans halved or chopped? Hope he doesn't have to look for another job by the end of lunch. It is very hard to sit still and since I am driving my friends crazy with my rapid-fire patter, we eat quickly and then go up to the Yayoi Masuko exhibit. I am going at 100 mph, so have trouble standing still long enough to focus on the art, although my attention is momentarily captured by the life-size silver rowboat covered with matching silver flaccid phalluses.

Run home to Henry. Since he still seems to be recovering from the first brisk walk, I give him a break — only ten blocks this time. Feed him dinner, and pull out a stack of CDs, then proceed to sing and dance my way from Mozart to Moss Hart, returning to my roots as an opera-turned-cabaret singer. Warble and whoop and execute several original jazz routines around the entire apartment for a few hours. Which makes me extremely hungry. Rummage through the overstuffed kitchen drawer, find the menu from my favorite Vietnamese restaurant and order five different dishes.

Food arrives after what seems like an eternity. Set out the Vietnamese dishes in a line running the length of the kitchen counters and eat my way around the room, standing up like a horse. The satiety mechanism is kaput; have no idea when I have eaten enough or too much.

Take Henry out for the last walk of the day, ignoring his efforts to hide his leash. Trim the outing down to a mere six blocks, but we are gone for almost an hour, since I have to stop and chat with everyone I know in the neighborhood, plus a few strangers who are also walking their dogs.

Around 11:00 p.m., after eighteen hours of perpetual motion, I take two Xanax and jump into bed. Turn on the TV and find Truffault's *Jules et Jim* in the original French. Decide to challenge myself by translating the dialog before reading the subtitles. By the time it's over, I'm wide awake. Start reading a fifteen-page article in my stack of bedside periodicals on the *History of Croatian Viticulture.* Finally make a to-do list for Sunday: Return half of yesterday's purchases to Saks, shop for groceries and cosmetics, and clean all major kitchen appliances as well as every inch of the countertops and floors with Comet and an electric toothbrush.

Everyone to whom I report these compulsive cleaning

outbursts begs me to come over to their house, but honestly, it's not me, it's just the Prednisone.

August 2012

Guinea Pig for a Good Cause

"I HAVE ONE SPACE left in a clinical trial," my doctor announced excitedly as soon as he entered the exam room for our weekly visit. "It's for Stage IV Melanoma patients — an immunotherapy drug which demonstrates remarkable results with less toxic side effects than traditional chemo."

"Sounds great," I said, before I even knew that it would require a year's commitment to bi-weekly infusions. "Sign me up!" I was proud and happy to be at the forefront of this new technology, and was delighted not only to be helping Dr. Wolchok in his research, but also to be helping other cancer patients. Because it was a Phase I trial, dosage, duration, side-effects, and efficacy were all unknowns. It made me feel as if I were making a contribution to an important body of knowledge.

At around $100,000 for a year's supply, these drugs were prohibitively expensive. But as a guinea pig in a clinical trial, their cost and all the concomitant tests were covered by the pharmaceutical company. In exchange, I had to show up for the two-hour IV infusion every other week, followed by an hour of monitoring for negative reactions. It took most of the day. First, I had to have my own blood drawn, have my doctor look at, and be satisfied with, the results. Then it took about two hours for MSK's in-house pharmacy to mix the drug and send it to the patient. At least once a month, instead of drawing just three vials of blood, the nurse showed up with a forest of test tubes in a plastic basket, all of which had to be filled, with results sent to the pharmaceutical company.

The first few weeks went smoothly. I arrived with my Kindle, read for a few hours, and answered emails on my phone. When I returned for each new infusion, the nurse would ask if there had been any reactions or side effects. "One," I answered after a few weeks. "I'm ravenous after the infusion. I not only eat my weight in the stash of graham crackers by the coffee machine, but also have to find a restaurant for a three-course meal within five blocks when I leave the hospital."

"Odd," said the nurse. "The majority of patients on this trial, experience *loss* of appetite. I think you're just experiencing anxiety."

After being told rather unsympathetically that my hunger was psychological, I stopped mentioning it.

On my next vampire blood-drawing day, I had about an hour to kill between filling the forest of test tubes and the start of the infusion. You're allowed to leave the hospital as long as they can reach you by cell phone and you can return quickly. Since Bloomingdale's was just six blocks away from the clinic, I decided I'd race up there to get a makeover, since I'd been looking a little pale.

I made a beeline for the Trish McEvoy counter and settled

myself on a stool. The lovely young make-up artist who took charge decided that I needed a dramatic look for evening. She began with my right eye, carefully applying black kohl eyeliner, a blended palette of increasingly smoky eye shadows — purple, forest green, and anthracite — and several coats of black mascara.

She had just finished that eye when my cell phone rang.

"Hi Aileen, this is Mary, your infusion nurse. We just got your blood results back; your liver enzymes are dangerously elevated. You have to return to the clinic immediately."

"Hmmm…potential liver failure? I see," I said calmly, since I always under-react to medical information until I understand the whole picture. "OK, I just hope you don't have to draw more blood! I'll be back at the hospital in about five minutes."

I turned to the sweet cosmetician who was growing increasingly pale during my conversation. I was still feeling fine, so I just turned to her and said, "I'm terribly sorry, but I have to dash back to the hospital." She doused some cotton pads with make-up remover and shakily handed them to me in a small bag.

Within minutes, I was back in the clinic, having stopped briefly in the bathroom to wipe off the multi-layered makeup. I mostly succeeded in smudging it. The nurse took one look at me and asked if someone had punched me in the eye during my lunch break. I said no, and explained that I had been at one of Bloomingdale's cosmetic counters experimenting with a dramatic evening look, when the hospital phoned and told me to return immediately.

Within a few days, the liver crisis was averted with high

doses of Prednisone, which further contributed to a voracious appetite.

While on the Phase I Trial, I experienced acute colitis and rashes, but it was all manageable and, unfazed, I made it through to the end. And, even though the drug initially shrank my tumors, they returned after a few months, so although it bought me some time, unfortunately that particular drug did not work for me.

Nonetheless, I was glad to have been able to contribute to the new body of knowledge about the drug; in this Act, the role of Research Scientist is played by Ms. Robbins. I never liked to dwell on my own individual illness, but this was different; it provided a much larger perspective.

The new drug was rushed through the FDA, and gained approval in record time. Within a few years, it being applied to several other types of cancer beyond melanoma, and was proving very effective, long-term, for many patients.

None of them, however, ever reported insatiable hunger during their treatment.

February 2012

Obstructed Justice

APRIL 3, 2015: CHECK into Memorial Sloan Kettering for bowel obstruction surgery to remove Stage IV melanoma tumors. Surgery goes well; clean outlines and my recovery is quick — home in six days, back at work in two weeks. Only painful part is the restricted diet.

Week of June 1: Strange rumblings in my stomach but am ignoring them.

Week of June 4: Rumblings get worse, are joined by severe cramps and then vomiting. Can't keep anything down, either liquid or solid, so check in to MSK's Urgent Care Center. An x-ray confirms an obstruction at the site of the resection. Not an uncommon result, but one which I never imagined would happen to me. I'm pleased that they diagnose it so quickly and I'm sure I'll be out in a few days.

June 5: Still in the hospital. In order to calm everything down, the doctor inserts a nasogastric tube through my nose which passes through the throat into the stomach. It vacuums out the contents of the stomach for the next four days. I watch as the yellow-brown bile chugs through a clear tube into a clear plastic bag. Discourage visitors.

June 6-19: On strict N.P.O. orders.

Nil Per Os is an elegant Latin phrase which translates to "nothing by mouth" — i.e., nothing liquid or solid can pass my lips. Am kept hydrated by the contents of two different IV solutions. I regard this as my Gandhi period.

June 17: Good news — this complete rest for the gut is helping; with nothing going in, the inflammation has been significantly reduced.

Nonetheless, my relentless optimism is put to the test. No mealtimes means no breaks from the day's activities (the highlight is walking twenty laps around the hospital corridors), nothing to punctuate my day. It's not just the meals that I miss; it's the chance to socialize, share good news, bad news, deep thoughts, and shallow gossip.

Attend many social events in the fifteenth-floor recreation center, but I'm just not into making a planter out of a hat. One day, the pastry chef from the Ritz-Carlton arrives with trays full of freshly-baked cupcakes and frosting, for a DIY cupcake fest. I walk in, smell the cupcakes, pivot, and walk out.

Also walk out on my roommate. Not that I don't like this adorable, perky young woman but she is on high doses on Prednisone *(See: Prednisone Princess Diaries)* and she and her husband spend all afternoon reading menus aloud, deciding what to order for dinner. A typical conversation goes as follows:

"Let's start with the bruschetta with wild mushrooms and an order of fried calamari."

"I don't know; I really feel like the zucchini strips and the antipasto platter."

"Okay, let's just order all of them."

"Good idea. What about pasta?"

"I'd like the Alfredo Florentine lasagna, although the wild boar ragu on pappardelle sounds good."

"Okay, both. Main course?"

I dash out the door, IV bags slamming against the pole.

June 19: My surgeon and I must decide whether surgery is necessary. This would entail re-opening the vertical incision from the recent resection, which risks creating more adhesions and another obstruction. Am vehemently opposed, especially since my new roommate, who was wheeled in this morning screaming in pain, just had her *third* obstruction surgery. We agree, no surgery.

June 20: Able to keep down liquids, so am released from the hospital — extreme jubilation!

June 20–July 5: First two weeks, tricky. Severe cramps about twenty minutes after I eat or drink, but liquids and solids stay down. Have to chew carefully and eat small portions. Diet is severely restricted. No gluten, no dairy, nothing hot or spicy, no raw fruits or vegetables, no alcohol, no caffeine, and as little fiber as possible. The newly crowned queen of compotes, I am also becoming expert at bone broth from scratch. Weight has dwindled to 100 lbs. Arms and legs scrawny, face gaunt, abdominal area still distended. Under other circumstances, this might have been my ideal weight, but given the circumstances, I look like Mrs. Potato Head.

August 24: Leave for a two-week vacation in the South of France with Peter and Armin. I can consume very limited amounts of gluten and dairy. Feeling great! I'm eating a wide assortment of Mediterranean fish, including langoustines so fresh and sweet, they bring tears to my eyes. Order ratatouille every chance I get; Riviera comfort food. Also eat my weight in meringues and *pâte de fruits*.

September 1: Tests show abdomen, pelvis and chest are clean. Am continuing to add in more food groups. Scan epicurean magazine and websites daily. Discover twelve new restaurants slated for opening and resolve to walk through their doors before the paint's dried.

November 2015

The Art of Receiving

WHEN I WAS A teenager, I was always a caretaker for family and friends. I even spent two weeks taking care of Tonya Bern Campbell, a glamorous French cabaret singer and friend of my parents, after her open-heart surgery. But when I was an adult, two caregiving experiences hit much closer to home.

My only child, a daughter, was diagnosed at age eleven with Stage IV Hodgkins. Two years of powerful chemo and radiation followed. At the time, I was a single mother, so I moved an extra bed into her room, and spent many nights there, holding cool compresses to her forehead and reading aloud long novels, such as *The Secret Garden*. We always had projects. One bitterly cold February night at around 3:00 a.m., after a particularly brutal wave of nausea, we decided we'd order some summer clothes from the newly arrived J. Crew catalog. We wanted to document that she could order skinny white jeans in size zero, since she had dropped to eighty-eight pounds. It was also a leap of optimistic faith, assuming that she would be alive and well enough to wear skinny jeans after Memorial Day.

I learned, very quickly, how to become an extension of the medical team, understanding how crucial it was for both patient and primary caregiver to participate in the protocol. At every visit, I would ask dozens of questions about the disease as well as the drugs and their side effects so that, after treatment, I could tell her doctor, "You have to decrease the dosage of this particular chemo drug or wait longer between infusions," or "you have to increase the anti-nausea drugs." One day when I walked into the clinic for my daughter's weekly treatment, her doctor pulled me aside and said, "May I ask you a favor?"

"Uh-oh," I thought, she was going to ask me to stop asking so many questions. Instead, she said, "If I'm ever hospitalized, will you be my patient advocate?"

A few years later, my second husband, who had been diagnosed with kidney cancer ten years earlier was diagnosed with Stage IV adrenal cancer. After five years, his nephrologist had become complacent, if not downright negligent. So, by the time the recurrence was discovered, it had metastasized to his lungs and spine. After viewing the chest x-ray, the new oncologist gave him six months.

What happened next in that doctor's office was extraordinary. Instead of his immediate reaction being one of disbelief, fear, and anger, he made two statements. First, he said how grateful he was for the eight years that he and I had shared. And second, he said one of the greatest lines I've ever heard. "Well, this certainly gives a new meaning to my ex-wife's alimony for life!" which he and I found hysterically funny, although the oncologist looked mystified by our gales of laughter.

Instead of making plans to visit Kathmandu or go on a whale hunt in Patagonia, we continued our life as usual, with him doing what he loved doing. There were many bleak moments, to be sure — the metallic taste in his mouth and his strong aversion to the smell of sautéing garlic or onions meant I had to radically change my style of cooking. And toward the end, the hallucinations brought on by the morphine were scary, since they seemed utterly real to him. When I visited him in the hospital one morning, he reported that I had just missed his ex-wife, his daughter, and her pet panther.

For the next few months, he edited his documentary research projects, watched endless hours of football alternating with movies, played with our dogs, enjoyed visits from friends and family, and watched our garden grow.

About five years ago, when I diagnosed with Stage IV melanoma, my immediate reaction was, "There must be some mistake. I don't get sick, I care for those who do."

I'm a care-giver, not a care-receiver by nature. My mother and grandfather were both Stoics. They never complained; it was a sign of weakness and dependence. There was nothing worse than to be thought of as needy.

I inherited that gene. So throughout all the procedures and protocols, it has been extremely difficult for me to ask for help. The last thing I wanted was to have my daughter re-live her own experience with cancer or be frightened about the outcome of mine. So, to this day, I downplay all pain. Even to nurses and doctors. After every surgery, I refuse morphine in the hospital, within twenty-four hours after the operation. And I think it's a trick question when the nurses ask me, "How would you rate your pain, on a scale of one to ten?" I always give a lower number.

My daughter shows up every day when I'm in the hospital, even though I tell her she doesn't have to. But once I get home, instead of turning to family and friends during the recovery, I feel much more comfortable hiring a professional caregiver. Then it becomes a business transaction and I am simply delegating.

"But we want to help," one friend said, sounding hurt. It was frustrating for my friends, who called or wrote frequently, not to be able to visit and take care of me, even if this meant just bringing or dropping off food. She explained that I was depriving them of a chance to demonstrate their friendship, that taking care of me would make them feel good.

After this summer's surgery, however, my attitude changed. I realized that I wasn't just depriving them; I was denying myself the comfort of community. So a few days after I came home from the hospital, I started inviting my friends over, one at a time. Sarah brought some amazing homemade chicken soup from Eli's, and Andrea dropped off wonderful poached salmon with dill sauce. I enjoyed every bite, and thanked them with a newfound ability to express gratitude.

July 2016

How to Be Your Own Patient Advocate

THE TUMORS WERE BACK. My doctors told me that I would need a third abdominal surgery. This was after three different courses of immunotherapy, two of which had seemed to work, but only for around four months.

Each of the abdominal surgeries required a long recovery, characterized by severe abdominal cramping, difficulty breathing, fatigue, weakness, and worst of all for me — a wildly restricted diet. Plus it meant I couldn't sing. As a former opera singer who transitioned into the wine and food world, not being able to eat and drink and sing meant a steep decline in quality of life.

But beyond the discomfort and deprivation, there was also the futility of it all. As the surgeon freely admitted when asked, there was a high probability that the constellation of small tumors near the top of my abdomen would grow back a few months after this surgery, as they had after each previous surgery.

But her argument was persuasive: cancer-ridden on

Wednesday, cancer-*free* on Thursday! So we set the date for surgery: January 4, 2017.

The week prior to surgery, I met with my main doctor and cut right to the chase. "I've decided not to undergo another surgery."

My doctor didn't miss a beat. "I respect your wishes; it's your body, and your decision," he said. "There's another, last-resort option we have: targeted therapy."

"Sounds great!" I said, with unbridled enthusiasm, even though I had no idea what it entailed. "When can I start?"

On February first, I was put on a protocol which involved a daily dose of five pills — four Dabrafenib and one Mekinist. At first, the side effects weren't bad; some chills, fever, nausea, but nothing that affected everyday life too badly.

By early March, however, my temperature was going past 102° and I was making monthly trips to the Urgent Care Center. Hypersensitive to the drugs, I was told I could switch from the daily dose to alternating weeks.

This wasn't much better. Nausea and severe muscle cramps were added to the chills, fever, and fatigue so, in addition to decreasing frequency, I made the case for decreasing the dosage. After all, I was fifty kilos, and how could they give the same dosage to other melanoma patients who weighed seventy-five or 100 kilos? So I got permission to reduce the dosage to two Dabrafenib.

Immediate increase in quality of life. My appetite returned, my energy level rose, and I wasn't taking my temperature every twenty minutes. I took on a new client, renewed my passport, and signed up for a class in the fall. But the physical anxiety was replaced by psychological anxiety. Having decreased both dosage and frequency, could this protocol still be effective?

My next PET scan was two months away. I got through those two anxious months with the help of a wonderful therapist at Memorial Sloan Kettering, whose specialty (who knew therapists could be so specialized?) was working with melanoma patients!

In May, I had the PET scan. There was no renewed growth; I was clean. I asked my doctor what I should do, going forward. He said that I should continue the daily dose "until I couldn't tolerate it anymore." Being an overachiever, my interpretation of that phrase was, "take it until you have a fever of 103° or can't breathe and have to go to the Urgent Care Center."

Time to redefine "tolerate."

My new definition stopped when my temperature went above 99°, when I experienced shortness of breath or fatigue. What was *tolerable* was inextricably bound to my definition of quality of life. I would rather be on a lower dose of this very new, potentially dangerous drug which could cause cardiac arrest and irreversible organ failure and live a happy, full life for *one* year, than be on a high dose and live a miserable life for two.

As I left the examining room, my doctor said to me, "Have a great summer. See you in the fall!" Amazing words, which meant I was on my own for four months — no blood drawing, no scans, setting my own protocol. I went to new restaurants, walked around four miles a day, spent weekends with friends and family outside the city, and went to a magical wedding in the South of France.

I had my next PET scan at the end of August. No new growth. Clean.

My doctor asked me what protocol I had designed for myself. I said, "It's pretty spontaneous: a few days on, a few days off, more if I'm still fatigued or warm." He put his fingers in his ears and went "*La-La-La-La!*" very loudly. He was kidding, of course, but he'd given me the power to partner with him in my own treatment. And I was grateful for the gift. Everyone in the room laughed, no-one more delightedly than me.

August 2017

nearer, I clamped my eyes shut and assumed the sarcophagus pose. She peeked in, saw me "asleep" and turned around. Even though I didn't hear the front door open or close, I assumed she had quietly let herself out.

Nope. After another half an hour, I heard a loud *crash!* She had flung one arms behind her while lying on the couch and somehow managed to knock all the photos off the end table, the tightly packed line of them toppling like a row of dominos. I yelled out in the loudest voice I could summon without herniating myself, "*What broke?*" to which, after a few minutes and some scrambling noises, she replied in a quasi-cheery voice, "Oh, nothing!"

I lay there for at least another half hour, unwilling to face any damage. Then I tiptoed down the hall and glanced furtively into the living room. No one in sight, but the room looked like it had been vandalized — coffee table and chairs moved, cushions askew. And not just the accent pillows but the couch's heavy seat cushions. All the framed photos were shoved randomly back onto the end table, although one was still on the floor. No sounds emanated from any other rooms. I proceeded cautiously into the kitchen.

The coast was clear.

I made myself a second cup of tea in about a minute and a half. Then I picked up the phone and, in less than an hour after the door had closed behind her, I hired a professional caretaker.

July 2016

Star of Brochure and Screen

WHEN I WAS DIAGNOSED with Stage IV melanoma six years ago, tumors were present in my limbs, my internal organs, and surprisingly, my left eye. This was discovered because I complained about a lot of floaters in this eye and, when the ophthalmologist performed a vitrectomy, which he described as "draining the swimming pool," the biopsy showed melanoma cells.

One of the graduate fellows at Memorial Sloan Kettering saw me first.

"This is unusual," he said, "the eye is considered a privileged site, and cells do not pass freely." I nodded, as if I knew what he was talking about.

"You should just have the eye removed," he continued cheerily, "that way, you won't have to worry about it spreading to the optic nerve and your brain."

Then my main doctor came in and said that ocular surgery certainly was the most efficient option — melanoma here today, gone tomorrow! Easy for them to say, it wasn't their eye.

"What other options do I have?" I inquired politely. Having major surgery, resulting in a large colored marble where my real eye used to be, didn't strike me as a viable option. "I still have a fair amount of vision in that eye."

"You could try radiation, although the success rate is only around fifty percent," said my doctor.

"That sounds pretty high to me," I responded. From what I knew about radiation, the procedure itself was almost completely painless, the side effects were minimal, and it required no marbles. "Definitely going with radiation over eye removal surgery."

"Fine, let's try radiation," agreed my doctor.

Three days later, I went in for the radiation simulation prep, which I assumed would be painless.

Once I was lying on my back on a narrow table, the technician placed a hot papier-mâché mask on my face and pressed it very hard into the edges of my skull to get as accurate and tight a face mold as possible. It covered my entire face except for small openings for eyes, nostrils and mouth; and extended under the chin, making it difficult both to breathe and to swallow. Then I was slid into an MRI machine, which determined how to line up the path of the ray. My head was locked into place with heavy clamps attached to the table, redefining the whole concept of claustrophobia.

The simulation ended once the papier-mâché had dried. The technician then ripped the mask from my face, taking some of the hairs along the temples and forehead with it. It also left an indentation all around the perimeter of my face. I would have to wear this mask, lined up with the radiation beams from the machine with my head in a vise, for twenty sessions, five days a week for four weeks.

Coincidentally, the day I had the mask made, I also was supposed to show up at MSK's Center for Integrative Medicine. Weeks before, I had agreed to be the subject of a photo shoot for their new acupuncture brochure. I had been attending their group acupuncture sessions at the Integrative Center for several months and had written a short enthusiastic testimonial, in response to their questionnaire, about how it had helped me.

So here I was, with a red groove all around my face and due for a photo shoot in forty minutes. I had just enough time to race home, where I slapped on makeup to try to hide the red marks. Didn't help much. I explained to the photographer the source of this ring of fire and asked him to be sure to air-brush it out. He agreed.

The real star of this shoot, of course, was Dr. Chan, the head acupuncturist, and the photographer snapped dozens of shots of him sticking needles in my ear as I lay on a white-sheeted table. I will always love this man, since at the end of the shoot he said, "I know you've had a hard day, Aileen, so I'd like to give you a free acupuncture session. Can you hang around for an hour?"

"Absolutely!" So I got to lie on a soft table in a dark room and listen to waves breaking against the shore and seagulls faintly crying while my stress melted away.

Dr. Chan and I were featured on the cover and inside the new color brochure, which was widely distributed. Print copies appeared in the waiting rooms throughout the MSK system. But most significantly, the cover shot was used in a slide loop that ran on their wall-mounted TVs throughout the main hospital and the satellites.

A few months later, I was recovering from abdominal surgery at the main campus and my daughter was doing laps with me around the tenth floor. She happened to glance up and, sure enough, the photo of her mother and Dr. Chan appeared on the wall-mounted TV screen.

"Oh my God, Mom, it's *you*!" she shrieked. I looked up and there I was with Dr. Chan. My daughter grabbed one of the passing nurses and pointed at me and then at the slide, exclaiming proudly, "Look, it's my Mom!"

Suddenly, it was all worth it.

September, 2015

Tips on Retinal Reattachment

MAY 12, 2015: GO in for a retinal re-attachment procedure with the top eye surgeon in the country. Surgery goes well, but must follow strict post-op instructions to keep my head down for five days, to allow the little silicon bubble to attach to the back of the eye. On the nurse's recommendation, I rent a special chair, like those massage chairs they have at nail salons, for a week.

Returning home after surgery, I position myself on the chair. Ten minutes later, I realize I can't tolerate this for one more minute. First, the face cradle is too small, especially with the protruding eye patch. Second, there is the sickening odor of leatherette framing my nose.

My "deluxe comfort package" also includes the "sleep solution", a small mattress covered in the same thin Naugahyde as the chair. From what I can glean from the poorly written instruction manual, the mattress with its own face cradle goes on top of the bed. I strap the attached band around my head, which sets off a piercing alarm every time my head moves out of the downward position for more than eight seconds. I notice a light pink spot at the top edge of the mattress, where the last patient must have drooled. I drop everything and call the rental company, demanding to speak to the manager.

"I am an extremely dissatisfied client," I continue, firmly. "I have just returned from eye surgery and have to keep my head down for five days but I won't last ten minutes on either of the torture devices that I rented from you for *two hundred and sixty-five dollars*."

The woman on the end of the phone makes some sympathetic clucking sounds, which only serve to infuriate me further. I raise my voice and in as cold and curt a tone as I can muster, I growl, "Forget the chair, which pitches me forward and presses against my face in a vise-like grip. The real problem is the sleeping apparatus: has anyone at your company ever *tried it?* Between the board, the face grip and the headband programmed to go off every eight seconds, it's worse than waterboarding!"

I am sure the manager, upon hearing this, will promise to pick up these contraptions within the hour and refund every cent. Instead, she starts giggling uncontrollably and much to my dismay, I join in. Sometimes a sense of humor can be a liability. Between snorts, she says she will pick them up tomorrow.

My only option now is to keep my head lowered on my own. In order to maintain this position (was I going to develop a widow's hump?) I spend hours writing "LOOK DOWN!" in capital letters in black magic marker on neon yellow Post-its. I position them at three-foot intervals on all the walls of my apartment, about two feet from the floor itself, as well as on furniture, mirrors, and doors. Consider putting one on top of the dog's head but he spends eighteen hours a day asleep under the dining room table, so he wouldn't be much of a help. Start wearing a visor with a Post-it dangling right over my eyes. Have to get through four more days. Am nervous about the outcome of the surgery.

May 13th: The Post-its have become invisible, a new wallpaper. Decide to re-position them directly on the floor, but am not supposed to bend, so I slide on my stomach like a snake from my bedroom to the kitchen, passing through two long hallways and the dining room, sticking them to the floor every three feet.

Since I am trying to keep up at work, I have to figure out how to type on my computer while standing up and keeping my head down. After several attempts, I succeed by balancing the keyboard on top of two shoeboxes.

May 15th: My daughter and four-year-old granddaughter come over for a visit. My granddaughter is delighted with all the Post-its, which she regards as a variation of an Easter egg hunt. She has a great time pulling them off the walls, mirrors, and furniture and asks if she can play this game the next time she comes over. She leaves before I tell her that the second part of the game consists of her putting all the Post-its back where she found them.

May 18th: Return to the eye surgeon, who says that the bubble has attached itself to the retinal wall and that the surgery is a success. On my way out, I tell the nurse to reconsider recommending the chair and mattress option to future patients, but offer to share my Post-its with anyone who wants them.

One year later: Even though I have the smoothest, most perfect retina attached to the back of my eye, due to the radiation, within the past several months I have lost all vision in that eye.

August, 2016

"You Look Mahvelous (for Someone with A Fatal Illness)"

Plus!

Special Bonus Section: Helpful Hints for Hospital Stays

THERE ARE SEVERAL PHRASES that well-intentioned friends, colleagues, and neighbors say to people with cancer and other life-threatening illnesses that make us want to shake them by the shoulders until their teeth rattle.

One that I anticipate with dread is, "Oh, but you look wonderful!" inevitably spoken with sincere astonishment when someone sees me a few weeks after surgery. What did they expect me to look like? A lurching corpse, with sunken eyes, black teeth, and ashen skin? First of all, I actively discourage visitors until I look presentable. But then if I look too good, sometimes people look at me suspiciously, as if I've made up my illness or the treatments.

I admit, I make an effort to look good because it makes me *feel* better. I get dressed up for any procedure, from a simple CBC to a PET scan to major surgery, and always take a large designer scarf with me to the Urgent Care Center (Memorial Sloan Kettering's name for the ER). This desire to look good, regardless of the occasion, was ingrained in me since childhood by Grandma Isabel, my mother's mother.

when you look good,
you feel good

Grandma Isabel was my fashion role model. She taught me how a lady should look when she steps out — not just out of the house, but out of the bedroom, as well. Although she and Grandpa Sam lived in a residential apartment in the St. Moritz Hotel with limited closet space, she had an extensive haute couture wardrobe which also included a wide selection of dressing gowns, silk robes, and quilted bed jackets.

Remembering her high standards, I suspect my desire to look good, even when hospitalized, is probably genetic. Of course, it's hard to look chic with a nasogastric tube strung between your nose and a vacuum machine, but, during those few days, the designer scarf does come in handy.

Bonus Section

Having spent a good deal of time in hospitals over the past seven years, I developed a brief list of helpful hints for women in the hospital or recuperating at home.

Hair: This is sacrosanct; always go to the beauty parlor to have your hair done *the day before surgery.* Have it cut, colored and blown dry. Even if you can raise your arms, it is difficult to wash your hair and blow it dry in the first few post-op days in your shared bathroom's open shower stall.

You should also invest in hair accessories — everything from scrunchies (originally spelled "scünci" with a totally affected umlaut, similar to the aberrant spelling of Häagen Dazs), to barrettes, headbands, clips, and combs. Different-sized scarves also work, although silky materials slip. And once you're venturing outside, always wear a hat.

As soon as you are mobile, head directly to the beauty salon. If you can't lean your head back in the shampoo chair, which is difficult after abdominal surgery, they will accommodate you, and let you lean forward.

I have tried over half a century to find a brilliant stylist who could cut my hair so perfectly that I could just blot it with a towel, fluff it with my fingers, get dressed and walk out the door. Not in this lifetime.

Fragrance: I am obsessed by scents. I want myself and my home or work environment to smell not just fresh and delicious, but welcoming and even enticing. I have two full shelves of perfumes and alternate between them depending on mood, season, occasion, and outfit.

Although the French used perfumes to mask unpleasant body odors, most Americans take personal hygiene seriously and shower daily, so perfume is used to attract and seduce. We are very sensitive to smell. I myself am hyperosmic.

It is especially important to create a good-smelling environment when in the hospital; not just for yourself but for everyone around you. Anything you can do to minimize unpleasant sick bed aromas will be appreciated by nurses, doctors, hospital staff, and visitors. After the most recent surgery, I discovered I was nauseated by some smell and couldn't figure out the source, since I was squeaky clean. It turned out to be coming from the antiseptic coating on the thin gauze strips that were used to pack the post-op abscesses. There was nothing I could do about it, but it was a big relief to identify the source, and I made sure to put a few drops of perfume on my torso (a safe distance from the packing).

Obviously, you have to be sensitive to the person with whom you share your hospital room; certain drugs make people hypersensitive to smells, and you don't want to take any chance of upsetting your roommate, who can tiptoe across the room while you're napping and hurl the offending scents into a wastebasket down the hall. Always ask your roommate before using any type of scent your body, the bed, or the air.

For bed linens: I spray a teeny amount of *eau de cologne* on pillows and mattress, which will quickly dissipate. (Sometimes I wait until I get home to do this.) There are sprays created specifically for bed linens; at the moment, my favorite is *Dans Mon Lit,* by master perfumer Bruno Jovanovic, part of the *Editions de Parfum* of Frederic Malle. Although the top note is rose, it is a complex scent, which integrates the scent of the stems, the leaves, and even the earth in which the roses grow. Makes me feel as if I am sleeping in a summer garden.

For the air: I love both diffusers and candles and often have both going at the same time at home (much to my daughter's dismay, who thinks I will burn the house down). Right now, I'm big on *Grapefruit* by Nest. The company describes it as "Pink pomelo and watery nuances blended with lily of the valley and coriander blossom." Mostly it smells citrusy and clean. And, since I doubt hospitals would permit you to burn candles, there's nothing wrong with a teeny diffuser, right near your bed. They make them without the oil, just the sticks. Again, be very sure it doesn't nauseate your roommate.

Corollary: Be careful with floral arrangements; anything with lilies or narcissus, for instance makes me sneeze, but I'd kill for freesia.

For your breath: I found a good line of toothpastes and mouthwashes, Oxyfresh. They have a non-flavored, non-alcohol-based mouthwash and a toothpaste for sensitive teeth which comes in very handy when chemo or immunotherapy drugs cause oral problems. You can get a battery-operated electric toothbrush for $11.99 at most major drugstore chains. And I always keep a purse-size minty breath spray by the bed.

Dress: While in the hospital, chances are very good that you will have to wear a hideous white gown with a small repetitive pattern in blue or black. Its major problem is that it opens in the back, with two ineffectual string ties that inevitably come undone. This means that everyone on the floor often catches unwanted glimpses of patients' flabby, dimpled, pimpled backsides. My solution is to slip a comfortable pair of pants (black, if possible) under the hospital gown.

Since it's usually cold in hospitals — on purpose to minimize the spread of germs — be sure to pack a beautiful warm scarf to drape around your shoulders. Scarves are more practical than sweaters since you will usually be hooked up to an IV pole, and can't navigate the sleeves.

Shoes: Although the hospital gives you weird disposable socks that have rubber ribbing on the bottom, I recommend bringing a flat shoe with some support and a rubber sole. I find these preferable to your own unattractive bedroom slippers, which, although they are easy to "slip" on, can also cause you to "slip."

Makeup: Grandma Isabel never left her bedroom, no less her house, without brushing her hair, blending a little dot of rouge on each cheek, and applying a fresh coat of lipstick. Keep a small hairbrush, a blush-on compact and a lipstick — could be conditioning gloss or just ChapStick — right near your bed. Reapply throughout the day.

Be careful not to apply *too* much make-up, since you don't want the doctors to perceive you as healthier than you are.

Listing these helpful hints have made me realize that I may be over-reacting to people telling me how good I look. The next time someone comments on my surprisingly healthy mien, instead of being insulted, I will feel complimented. "It's all thanks to Grandma Isabel," I will graciously reply

December 2018

Festina Lente

I'M A FOURTH GENERATION native New Yorker. I talk fast, I walk fast, and if I'm not mindful, unfortunately I eat fast. For many years, I had to move at the speed of light to take care of my family, my business, my dogs, and myself.

To manage it all, I'd wake up at 6:15 a.m., speed-brush my teeth with an electric toothbrush, throw on my clothes, run the dogs, feed them, and then fly out the door again, banging on the elevator button multiple times because some small irrational part of my brain thought it would come faster. I'd make a mad dash to the subway and charge down the stairs in a syncopated rhythm. If the train was already in the station I would hurl my body into the nearest car, while apologizing profusely to everyone on all sides.

I'd get to my gym by 7:30, work out for an hour, take a quick shower, stop at the deli for yogurt and be at my office before 9:00 where I'd remain, working on overdrive, until I left at around 7:00 p.m.

For decades, I kept up this up, never wondering about what it might be doing to my body or mind. I was healthy; in fact, my blood pressure was so low — eighty over sixty — that one doctor asked me if I were hibernating.

Then in 2011, completely asymptomatic, I was diagnosed with Stage IV melanoma. I had immediate surgery followed by years of immunotherapy, radiation, more surgery, and most recently, targeted therapy. Suddenly the whole rhythm of my life had to change. I was no longer a whirling dervish. This last round of therapy caused shortness of breath as well as muscle and joint soreness. I couldn't race-walk, no less run.

When the melanoma invaded my left eye, I underwent radiation that fried the optic nerve, so I lost all vision in that eye. Being a Cyclops seriously affected my peripheral vision as well as my depth perception. No more running down subway steps, no racing to catch a bus, no leaping over curbs to avoid puddles or snowdrifts. And no more coffee from the downstairs deli.

I used to pop in for a steaming hot cup of coffee from one of their giant silver urns on my way to work. There's always a line for coffee, mostly comprised of local construction workers. I was pouring myself a coffee one morning and wondering why my cup was still empty when the man next to me cursed loudly and I realized that the stream of boiling hot coffee was completely missing the cup, and was landing instead on this poor man's work boots.

Even now, five years later, I am still adjusting to this vision loss and struggling to adapt to a slower pace. At Bloomingdale's this week, I was reminded again of how badly I've adjusted. I took the elevator to the third floor; escalators are dangerous, since I'm never sure when the step rises or lowers. I was returning an item which looked a lot better in the mirror at the store. But first, I asked one of the salesmen where the ladies' room was. "Oh, let me take you there!" he said and started walking briskly down a narrow central aisle where five tall mannequins were lined up, six feet apart.

The mannequins must have stood on my blind side because, all of a sudden, I heard a loud *crash* as one of them clattered to the floor. That might not have been so bad, but the poor thing landed on her hands, and about eight of her ten slender fingers snapped and flew off in all directions.

Startled by the noise, the salesman ran back, dropped to his hands and knees and scurried around trying to collect the errant digits before anyone tripped over them. It was all very Addams Family.

The evil part of me was secretly sorry that the mannequins hadn't been one foot closer to each other, in which case they would have *all* come crashing down like fashion dominoes. But I swept that thought away and instead focused on the mantra which my best friend Peter had given to me after the radiation: *Festina lente.* Since I've forgotten my three years of Brearley Latin, I thought it meant something like, *Have a party during Lent.*

But Peter informed me that it means, "Make haste slowly." Words to live by.

I suspect the incident was captured on Bloomingdales' security cameras. By now, there is probably a photo of me with a circle and diagonal line bisecting my face in the staff room of every floor. I'm going to steer clear of the store for a while and focus, instead, on my new mantra:

Festina lente, festina lente, festina lente.

November, 2018

VIII

I'm Still Here. When Do We Eat?

Life is too short not to eat well

~Eataly

A Day in the Life of a Foodie

DECEMBER 13, 2002: WOKE UP on Friday with a craving for waffles with Toblerone. Ran into the kitchen, chased by barking spaniels. Found the waffle mix but remembered that Ariel had eaten the remainder of the gigantic triangular Toblerone bar when she stopped by for dinner after Spanish class earlier this week.

Decided I didn't have time to make waffles, would just have a multi-grain English muffin and apricot jam instead. Reached for the eighteen-oz. glass jar of Sarabeth's Peach-Apricot Legendary Spreadable Fruit and tripped over the tri-color spaniel which made the large jar slip out of my hand and crash to the floor, splintering into dozens of pieces. I position myself on top of the orange mess, so the dogs don't eat it along with shards of glass.

Takes about two rolls of paper towels to clean up the sticky mess and I'm sure there are little flecks of glass still hidden in corners and under the fridge, but mopping the floor will have to wait until I get home. Have an eye doctor appointment at 8:30 a.m.

The doctor informs me that I have narrow angle glaucoma, which requires immediate surgery, since it can result in (as she gently puts it) "permanent blindness." She lists a few other symptoms: Nausea (in my family, nausea is not a symptom; it's a lifestyle); blurred vision, halos around lights, and so on. When the nurse asks about a date to schedule the surgery, I reply rather obnoxiously, "immediately if not sooner," thinking she'll say, *Okay, how's March 3rd?*

But instead she says, "Monday at 8:00 a.m."

I leave the doctor's office a little shaken. Some people might want a drink when they get bad news; I get peckish. I start looking around for the nearest deli or restaurant. Find a French bakery on Lexington Avenue and get a slice of almond brioche and a skim cappuccino. Eat and drink while speed-walking to the subway, which results in spillage, on both the shearling coat and the cashmere scarf. Toss the remaining coffee and brioche into a garbage can before boarding the train in order to avert any more accidents.

Get off the subway at 42nd Street for a 10:00 a.m. meeting with my main client, the Trade Commission of Spain, in the Chrysler Building. Spend two hours reviewing a final draft of my agency's Year End Report for *Brandy de Jerez*. My creative team has put in a customized black binder, embossed with the *Brandy de Jerez* logo in red. It is an inch-and-a-half thick, with separate printed tabs, brimming with photos, charts, graphs, lists, samples of promotional materials, conclusions, and recommendations for the future.

The notebook took weeks to assemble. Once I get their approval on this version, I have to make up a dozen copies, since each of the participating brandy producers gets one, plus a few go to the *Consejo Regulador* in Spain, and some stay in the New York office. It is incredibly detailed and reading even one chapter is a surefire cure for insomnia. I was tempted to bury a risqué photo somewhere in the middle of it, just to see if anyone actually read it all the way through, but my partner talked me out of it.

My client is delighted by its polished appearance, as well as its heft. I leave, thinking I should be happy that they were happy, but instead I think, I just spent three eighty-hour weeks putting together a book that no-one will read. Is this how I want to spend my life?

The immediate solution to this existential crisis is to stop and have a cappuccino and a carrot muffin. Added to the two cups of barely potable Mister Coffee that I downed during the meeting, I am buzzing around, and take the subway steps two at a time. Remember the magnet on my fridge which says, "Drink coffee. Do stupid things faster with more energy!" Make a note to take Aveda's Caffeine-Free Comfort Tea, which Kelly sent me for my birthday, to the office.

Am soon back at my office, and am starving, but scared of eating too much, since I have my personal training session at Equinox at 1:00 p.m. and I don't want to get cramps or listen to liquids slosh in my stomach while executing a Pilates sequence. Stop in the Korean deli in my building and buy a Dannon peach yogurt smoothie. Figure that will hold me.

Unscrew the cap and take two large gulps, but notice

immediately, that it tastes funny. Thin and watery, more sour than usual. Look inside and see green and grey mold growing on the sides of the container. Scream and fall over my desk, knocking over the ugly ceramic mug branded with a client logo, stuffed with twenty non-functioning pens and pencils. Michael, the office manager, rushes in. I show him the green-grey mold inside the yogurt container and tell him to call Peter to start writing my obit. He laughs and returns to his desk.

Indignantly, I race out the door, storm into the Korean deli, and stand in front of the cash register where I pantomime that I have been poisoned, by holding the yogurt in the cashier's face in one hand and clutching my throat with the other, while emitting choking noises. The cashier refuses to grasp that this is a life or death situation which, I point out verbally, is due to a past-dated dairy product that I bought in her store. So I yell, "I've been poisoned! This container is full of grey green mold and if I don't die from that, then I will break out in horrible hives all over my body because I am wildly allergic to all forms of penicillin!"

"Oh," she remarks calmly while making change for another customer. "Want money back? Here, $2.50."

"No, I don't want money; I want health and long life! Don't want to die premature death due to yogurt poisoning from downstairs deli!"

She turns to the next customer. I take the $2.50 and leave.

I go upstairs, pick up my messages, and then take off for the gym. Am a few minutes late for Michelle, my trainer, since I stop to talk to my friend Astrid in the locker room while I'm changing into my workout clothes. She is this crazy German girl with gold nipple rings and multi-color tattoos on her privates.

Almost didn't recognize her, since she changed her hair color from pink to blue (the tattoos were the give-away). She makes the mistake of asking me how I am. I give her a quick overview of my day so far, full of irony which I am sure she will find highly amusing, but instead, she bursts into tears. Have to spend a few minutes calming her down, but don't actually hug her, since am nervous about her nipple rings catching on my La Perla leotard.

Michelle starts me off on the treadmill, working up to a speed of five-and-a-half mph, with an incline of three. Am barely able to breathe. She asks me how I am, on a scale of ten, zero being comfortable, ten being unendurable pain. I say twenty. I offer to pay her extra if she lets me get off the treadmill and we can spend the rest of the hour at Dos Caminos or anywhere they serve margaritas and chimichangas.

She lets me get off the treadmill but refuses to let me go to the restaurant. Instead, she says we will spend the rest of the session kick-boxing. I am soon wishing I were back on the treadmill. Kick-boxing takes enormous strength, focus and coordination. After twenty minutes, I feel like I am rapidly approaching cardiac arrest and convince her to let me spend the remaining time having her stretch me.

Go back to the office, where Michael threatens to hide the Keurig coffee capsules. Spend a few hours writing ad copy, a newsletter, and answering a vast number of emails which breed like rabbits in my absence.

I leave the office at seven to run over to Boqueria, where I'm meeting my quartet of great friends, whom I met through my husband Alex. They had all worked with him in Spanish media, about thirty years ago, and have remained close friends with each other ever since. I was very fortunate because they brought me into their close circle when I came into Alex's life, and I soon became their friend in my own right.

Boqueria is an excellent tapas restaurant near my office, which I patronize so often that I've memorized the menu. We are all hungry so, along with a pitcher of Sangria, we order *Jamón Ibérico* (from special black pigs, fed mostly on acorns); sautéed spinach with pine nuts, garlic, and golden raisins; blistered *shisito* peppers; *patatas brava*, crispy and spicy; *pulpo a la plancha* (grilled octopus with fennel); *tortilla Española*; two kinds of *croquetas*; *pan con tomate; gambas al ajillo*; and my all-time favorite, bacon-wrapped dates stuffed with almonds and Spanish blue cheese. When the plates are empty, nobody can breathe and we pass on dessert.

Stop at the deli to pick up a small bar of Toblerone, since tomorrow is Saturday, a perfect day to make waffles, which I regretted all day having missed for breakfast. Thinking about something sweet makes me want a little something right now to round out the meal, so I go into the kitchen and make myself a small bowl of raspberry and chocolate sorbet (never ice cream, too rich), to clear the palate.

Am *so* looking forward to breakfast.

December 2002

Please Don't Eat the Centerpiece

ONE DAY LAST WEEK, my friend and fellow *Dame d'Escoffier*, Marsha, interviewed me for her blog. Every day she has a different topic and that day's topic was *beauty*. I am such a shallow, vain person that my first thought was of the Chanel counter at Saks. But I choked that response back and came out with some nonsensical but profound-sounding quote about beauy being, "whatever removes us from the mundane, and elevates the spirit."

Then she told me about the white Scandinavian bowl with perforations near the rim on her table in her apartment in Paris, into which she randomly tossed a few lemons and oranges one morning. She said every time she walked by that bowl, she was struck by how beautiful the fruit looked in it. It gave her enormous pleasure for days, just to look at that bowl.

"Ah!" I said excitedly, "that reminds me of one of the centerpieces I created for a dinner party!" and I proceeded to recount one of my favorite Peter stories.

I was giving a formal dinner party and wanted to create a

special centerpiece for the table in my very grown-up dining room, which has an elaborate, old-fashioned crystal chandelier hanging from the middle of the ceiling (which was there when I moved in).

I spent a lot of time on that particular arrangement. First, I decided on a fall color scheme with shades of red, purple, and scarlet. At the market, I bought appropriate fruits, starting with dark purple Ribier grapes and beautiful deep red pears: Red Bartlett, Red Anjou, and the more petite Forelle and Seckel. To these I added several dark red applies — Red Delicious, Braeburn, Macoun — and finished with two pomegranates. At home, I arranged these fruits with great care on a base of deeply colored autumn leaves which Ariel and I had gathered that afternoon from Central Park.

Since I had recently finished a shoot for the cover of a cookbook that I had co-authored, I was familiar with a few tricks of the food-photography trade. For example, to enhance color and shine, the stylist sprayed the food with glycerin. I didn't have any glycerin handy, so I used peanut oil instead. I had several candles of different heights around the centerpiece since I wanted the skin of the fruits and the leaves to reflect the candlelight.

I spent an inordinate amount of time oiling every little grape, every apple, pear, and pomegranate. I went on to oil every single leaf lying on one of Grandma Isabel's heavy silver platters.

Pleased with my efforts, I then focused on preparing the five courses: Oysters on the half shell with mignonette sauce (served in the living room); a salad of endive, Roquefort, mâche and spiced toasted walnuts; a crown roast of lamb with roast potatoes, glazed carrots, sautéed sugar snap peas. Before the dessert course of cheese and a *tarte tatin*, there was an intermezzo of a Campari-Grapefruit Sorbet (I was working for Campari USA at the time). In order to have this be as fresh and vibrant as possible, I had to excuse myself from the table, and go into the kitchen to squeeze several grapefruit, then toss the juice into my ice cream maker with simple syrup and Campari. This took around fifteen minutes.

When I returned to the table, the first thing that I noticed was that where the plump shiny bunch of Ribier grapes had been, there was now a brown skeletal stalk with little bare branches. I looked around the table and noticed that my best friend Peter was making odd smacking sounds with his lips. I had all I could do not to drop my tray of Campari sorbet.

"You ate the centerpiece?" I shrieked.

"The grapes looked so delicious, they were positively glowing; I just had to sample some," replied Peter, smiling.

"Didn't they taste peculiar?" I asked.

"Well, there was something a little oily and slick about the skins," he said thoughtfully.

"Yes, there certainly was," I retorted — "they were coated in pure peanut oil. It took me twenty minutes to oil all the fruit, including every single damn grape."

He made more smacking sounds and took several sips of water, in a vain attempt to wash away the coating of oil that covered his mouth, teeth, gums, lips.

That was the last time Peter touched one of my centerpieces.

Important Post Script: In a fit of fact-checking, I asked Peter about this incident, telling him how I remembered it. Peter recalled it clearly, but differently. Here's his comment:

"You may wish to add that one or two of the other dinner guests also started wiping their mouths when the secret of the peanut oil was revealed, but of course, I was the only one who actually took the rap. *But I was not the only one who ate the centerpiece!*"

October, 1992

Campari-Grapefruit Sorbet

Ingredients

- 1/2 cup water
- 1/2 cup sugar
- 2 cups fresh squeezed grapefruit juice
- 2 ounces, Campari

Make a sugar syrup by dissolving the sugar in the water, bringing it to a boil and simmering for 5 minutes. Let it cool, then mix it with the grapefruit juice and the Campari. Freeze in an ice cream machine or put the liquid in a bowl in the freezer. When almost frozen, put in a blender to dissolve ice crystals and achieve a smooth consistency.

Serves 4

Disaster Dinner Party

I WAS IN THE wine and food business for decades, so if I'm not eating a marvelous meal, then I'm thinking about marvelous meals I've had in the past, or about ones I'd like to have in the future. I don't give many dinner parties, but those that I do give, I start planning, weeks ahead.

I hadn't given a dinner party in a long time, but I was part of a group of serious foodies who invited each other to our houses on a fairly regular basis, and it was my turn.

It was a party of eight. One couple wrote cookbooks; another man was the Vice President of Banfi Estate Wines; the third couple were both wine writers, and the husband of the fourth couple was a chef.

The entire week before: Spend every evening cleaning the house, polishing silver, checking china and wine glasses, service plates, serving pieces, vases, napkins. Took Grandma Isabel's embroidered tablecloth out of the linen closet along with the oversized linen napkins. Thank heavens everything still is encased in dry cleaner's plastic, wrinkle-free. I break out in a rash if I even pick up an iron.

Thursday evening after work: Go to the butcher at Grace's, a special gourmet market. Engage him in a heated debate on what to serve. Finally decide on buffalo ribeye steaks. I will go with Niman Ranch, a very special meat wholesaler in Northern California which "raises livestock traditionally, humanely and sustainably to make the best tasting all-natural meat in the world." The butcher nods towards the free-standing cold box in the corner, where all the specialty cuts are kept. I immediately find the Niman Ranch individually sealed steaks and pile eight of them into my cart.

Lug them home, but am excited; now comes the creative part, hunting for a brilliant way to prepare them. Am about to go online when best friend Peter calls. I tell him about the buffalo steaks and he says they would be complemented brilliantly by lingonberries. I go back to Grace's, since I remember seeing that they stocked this when I was searching for pomegranate jelly on an earlier trip. I was right. Buy three large jars of lingonberry preserves.

Go back online to search *Buffalo Recipes*. There are about fifty-eight different sites, many of which are recipes (discounting *Buffalo Wings).* Some are very odd, offering recipes for ostrich, alligator, woodchuck, and rattlesnake. I am overwhelmed and decide that the best way to proceed is to e-mail Niman Ranch directly, and ask what the purveyor would suggest. Am curious, since I have already checked out Niman's website, and although I found recipes for beef, pork and lamb, I didn't see any for buffalo. Figure they don't sell as much of it, so they didn't bother posting separate recipes. I spend over two hours perusing the various sites, printing out fifteen recipes. Learn about every aspect of a bison's life, as well as insights into the culture of the Indians on the Great Plains. My eyes are crossing out of fatigue, but I am thrilled that I am getting some authentic and delicious buffalo recipes. Around midnight, I receive the following e-mail back from Frankie of Niman Ranch:

> *Aileen, I'm curious about where you bought Niman buffalo steaks? The reason you could only find beef, pork, and lamb is because that's all we produce! No buffalo! I hope someone is not marketing these incorrectly as ours! ~Frankie Whitman*

I go to the fridge, look closely at packages. Frankie is right. I have bought eight *beef,* not buffalo, steaks. Take two Tylenol and throw the fifteen buffalo recipes in the wastebasket.

Friday, one day before the party: Before heading down to the office, dash across the street to Grace's to return the eight ribeyes and three jars of lingonberry jam. Buy a double rack of lamb instead. Then go to the wholesale flower district on West 28th Street, buy five dozen pale pink roses with red edges and an assortment of greens and baby's breath. Leave work early, to arrange flowers. Start sneezing from the roses. Take an antihistamine.

Saturday: Go to my neighborhood wine store, buy two bottles Taittinger, two bottles Chablis Premier Cru for the first course; four bottles Grgich Hills Zin for the lamb. Go to

Citarella, buy ten stone crab claws, four dozen oysters, two lbs. boiled shrimp for first course.

Go back to Grace's, buy vegetables: salsify, baby *courgettes*, baby beets (gold), baby beets (candy striped), Russian fingerling potatoes. And stock up on fruits for plating desserts: raspberries, blackberries, and strawberries. Go to Payard, buy lemon tart, four kinds of macaroons, plus Valrhona chocolate in order to make my own bitter chocolate mousse.

Jump in shower. Race out to kitchen to start food prep — it's now around 5:15 p.m. and guests are set to arrive at 7:30. Need candied walnuts for the mache, endive, and blue cheese salad. Toss walnuts in walnut oil (a bit heavy handed) and a tablespoon of maple sugar; throw them under the broiler for a few seconds to toast.

The phone rings and I run to the opposite wall to answer it — it's one of the guests asking if there's anything he can bring. I haven't been on the phone for more than twenty seconds when I smell something burning; realize the sugar and oil from the nuts have caught on fire. Open door to broiler, huge flames leap out. Close the door, figure, I'll wait a few minutes and it will burn itself out.

Wait a few minutes, re-open door of oven; flames are higher, wilder, shooting out from the back of stove as well as the front. Calmly call down to the doorman and ask him for the large fire extinguisher they keep in the basement. Black smoke is billowing through the kitchen. Drag dogs into the dining room and close the gate. Open back door to common stairwell, plus every window in every room; turn on all air conditioners.

Hear high pitched deafening noise — the smoke has

triggered the fire alarm in the back hall. Neighbors start to call. Handyman and super are away (it's a weekend), so Bobby the doorman has to leave his post to bring the fire extinguisher up to my apartment. Bobby opens it up full throttle, and sprays billows of greenish-grey foam over the entire stove, inside and out, totally saturating all surfaces. He also sprays the walls and the floor. Fire is out. Bobby goes back to his post.

Barbara, head of the co-op, bursts in the back door; she is worried that the fire *looks* like it's out, but has traveled inside the back wall, and the whole apartment building will soon burst into flames. She wants to call the fire dept. I beg her not to, knowing that firemen often enter the site of a fire, rip doors off their hinges, take axes to walls, and flood all surfaces with high pressure jets of water. I tell her that seven people will arrive at my house for a very important dinner party in an hour and a half.

She is willing to compromise; calls the super at his country house instead. They have a fifteen-minute conversation, during which time she periodically peers down into the back of the stove and feels the heat on the wall. He seems comfortable that the crisis has passed. It is now 6:15. Barbara stays to help me wash the kitchen, which is truly a disaster area. All my little plastic containers of fresh herbs, which I left on top of the stove, have melted and would look right at home in a Dali painting. All my Dixie cups with carefully measured ingredients are filled with soot. I throw them all out and start again.

Sainted neighbors, Lee and Sharon, call up on the house phone (they heard the fire alarm) and offer not only to let me use their oven, but also to use their entire apartment. Definitely an option, but then again, so is Chinese delivery. Thank them, but refuse their kind offer.

Spend next half hour scrubbing away the green-grey chemical foam with sponges and a mop. As I'm wringing out the mop, I notice that there is an excessive amount of water on the floor in front of the sink; realize that there is a *leak* coming from the main pipe under the sink. The pipe has a crack in it. Put a large pan on the floor to catch the water.

First two guests arrive. I am still in jeans and a t-shirt, face and arms covered with soot and grey foam. Decide the first course will take place in the living room. I give them the two bottles of Champagne and platters of oysters, crab, and shrimp.

Manage to clean the oven enough to put the crown roast in. Pray that the lamb will not absorb whatever foam I missed. Make a sauce from my previously homemade veal stock, which was safely tucked away inside the fridge, and Madeira, hoping it will mask whatever burnt aromas may be permeating the oven.

More guests arrive. Race in to bathroom; scrub face and arms; throw on clean clothes. Sit down in living room for five minutes, have a glass of Champagne. See Henry, my blonde spaniel, taking a crab claw off the coffee table. Wrestle it out of his mouth and return to kitchen; lock both dogs back in the kitchen. Decide not to make the chocolate mousse. Have another glass of Champagne.

Stir-fry the baby vegetables with some ginger and garlic, while I parboil the baby potatoes before throwing them in the oven with the lamb. Remaining guests arrive. Tell them dinner will be a little late — like tomorrow. Everyone laughs, except for me.

Actually manage to sit down at the dining room table at around 9:30 p.m. After several bottles of Champagne and wine, no one thinks anything tastes peculiar. Serve dessert around 11:00, Cognac around midnight. Might as well be in Barcelona.

Must invite Barbara, Lee, and Sharon over for dinner sometime soon.

March 1993

Pastrami Queen

I STOPPED BY MY mother's after work, had two glasses of Riesling and some salt and vinegar potato chips, and then took the crosstown bus home. Got off on 79th and Lex. and was on my way down to 71st Street when I passed, for the hundredth time, The Pastrami Queen on 76th & Lex. I always just keep on walking, since I think, *Really? How could there be a decent pastrami anything on the Upper East Side?* But, drawn by insatiable curiosity and free-floating anxiety after spending three hours with Millie, I ventured inside.

None of the countermen were Jewish. They were all Pakistani. So I said, "What makes *this* the Queen of Pastrami?" To which one of the guys replied, "Have a taste. Very very good. We make it ourselves." And I thought, how could they know how to make pastrami? It's shocking enough that the old Jewish countermen at the historic Jewish deli, Katz's on the lower East Side, have been replaced by Hispanics.

Rajiv cuts several slices, puts them on a piece of wax paper and hands it over the counter to me. Hmmm. Pretty good. But everything always tastes better when it's a free sample given to you by the man behind the counter — it's fresh, it's hot, it's juicy. Then I feel guilty not buying something when he had just given me such a generous sample, so I order a pastrami on rye to go. It comes to $15.27. Even though they're paying an Upper East Side rent, I thought, *it should be eight inches high to justify that price*, but it's only about four and doesn't even come with a side of coleslaw. Just a new pickle, which turned out to be far too new.

So I walk out of the Pastrami Queen and unwrap the sandwich right there on Lexington Avenue and 76th Street and bite into the center of the sandwich. You know how they pile the meat, so that it resembles a bell curve, with the most meat in the middle, tapering off to the sides? So the best bite is that first bite, right in the middle, minutes after it's been sliced, when it's still hot, before the rye bread loses its shape and texture.

Total bliss. Just the right proportion of meat to fat, enough mustard, and soft but not soggy bread. I pretend to stare in the window of the candy store next door, so I can enjoy that perfect bite at that exact moment in time. I think, this is what a crazy person does: Stands in front of a window of a closed store to eat a hot pastrami sandwich in the middle of Lexington Avenue at nine o'clock at night. But that bite is so good that I didn't care if anyone thinks I'm a crazy person standing in front of a candy store eating a sandwich on Lexington Avenue; nothing exists in my world except that one perfect bite.

Pastrami Queen, indeed.

August 2018

The Epicurean Gene

I WAS HOPING TO feel a lot wiser at this age. But if I am not replete with wisdom, at least being alive for several decades has given me perspective. I don't sweat the small stuff. It doesn't matter if you do badly on an exam, if your boyfriend dumps you, if your sweater shrinks in the dryer. What matters is that you have treated people with kindness, that you have listened to them, made them feel better, and made them laugh. What matters is that you've added something to the lives around you.

Along with these lofty ethical and moral tenets, I also want to pass along to my daughter and my granddaughter a passion for what I consider the great pleasures of life. The arts, travel, reading, and of course, *food.*

But I was aware that my obsession with food might make Ariel want to rebel against it, the way my mother rebelled against *her* mother's obsession with fashion. Not that I made gourmet meals when it was just the two of us; like any working mother, I had a set repertoire of child-approved dishes: Roast chicken; lamb chops with hoisin sauce; LeSueur frozen *petits pois* with butter and a splash of good balsamic vinegar; veal and spinach loaf, and baked potatoes. With these, we scraped out the flesh and rolled the skins up with a dab of butter to make 'cigars'. But we were much more adventurous when we went out, and she was always willing to experiment with new cuisines and new ingredients. What she didn't like were the meals I made for company — "too fancy, too rich, too many ingredients."

I have to admit, however, that her favorite childhood meals were not from my house, but from Sarah Bond's. One of my best friends, Sarah was the mother of Daisy, one of Ariel's best friends since nursery school. She was from the UK and had a slightly different set of recipes that Ariel adored. Her favorite was Sarah's Shepherd's Pie. Her second favorite was a salami sandwich on a French baguette.

There were two dishes of mine that not only survived my daughter's childhood, but stayed adult favorites of hers as well. In fact, she will occasionally show up on a weekend morning and ask me to make them for her. One is a shredded carrot, apple, and tuna salad in a vinaigrette with a touch of mayo; the other is very soft creamy scrambled eggs with cheese and fresh dill. She has asked me for the recipes several times, but I do them differently each time, so it's impossible to pin them down.

I also taught her the Golden Rule of Restaurant Dining: Sharing. You have to offer a bite of whatever is on your plate, even if it is really delicious, to everyone at the table. This is not always possible, of course, if it's an appetizer portion or a tapas, because then you won't have any left for yourself, but then just order a second one. It was the way my father taught us to eat, although many people blanch at this, considering it a barbaric and unsanitary. My husband Alex, for instance, who grew up with three siblings, practically built a fort around his plate, ready to stab you with his fork if you came within inches of his dinner.

I understood my father's reasoning perfectly. He wanted us to taste as many dishes as possible, so we would experience more of the menu and expand our epicurean horizons. Which is why it makes me a little crazy when I take my family out to a new restaurant and Ariel and Justin order the same appetizer or entrée. They are used to my glowering, however, and pay no attention to it. But ultimately I'm happy if they enjoy their meal. Anyway, if it's a really good restaurant with lots of interesting dishes, I can always go back with one of my serious foodie friends, such as Gordon.

I was wondering what type of eater my granddaughter Sage would be, but I didn't have to worry. When she was three, her favorite dish was rice and beans (she has a Latina babysitter). At four, she loved olives. At five, she developed a passion for sushi. For snacks, she loves crispy seaweed.

For her seventh birthday, we went to Spartina, down in the Meat Packing District, since she loved oysters on the half shell. I ordered two dozen for the table, thinking she'll have about two or three. She kept pace with her parents and me, who quickly downed half a dozen apiece. When there were six left, she politely asked if she could have them. Astonished, we agreed.

Now I just have to find a restaurant that prepares authentic French frogs' legs, like the ones I'd ordered at the Stork Club on my sixth birthday.

I know Sage will adore them.

February 2019

Acknowledgments

BEYOND THANKS TO THE two fixed stars of my life, Ariel K. Fantasia and Peter Kazaras. Although I originally just asked them to fact-check, since they appear in a number of the essays, they went far above and beyond to make invaluable editorial contributions.

To Brook Ashley, not only for her undying support and enthusiasm about my writing, but also for her decades-old ability to make me laugh as much as I make her laugh. Next time, I'll include more of our email exchanges.

To my father, Louis J. Robbins, for having passed along the humor gene; my mother, for having been a very good audience (she couldn't tell a joke if her life depended on it, but she laughed spontaneously every time my father told one, no matter how many times she'd heard it). And my sister, Jane Marla Robbins, who also inherited the humor gene, and, being four years older, served as an excellent role model. At any performance, we always shriek with laughter at the same lines or shticks. She has a good sense of humor about herself, and coached me in my first stand-up comedy routine, which included some material from her life.

My editor, Constance Costas, who has supported me from the first day she wandered into the writers' workshop at Shakespeare and Co.

Judi Hannan, an excellent editor, who didn't work on this book as a whole, but helped me write multiple drafts of many of the essays included. She became my Visible Ink Mentor in 2013. And huge thanks to the principals of Visible Ink, who read my submissions every year since I first joined, and included me in the past six *Anthologies*: Judith Kelman, Founder and Executive Director; Greg Kachejian, Artistic Director (who directed "The Prednisone Princess Diaries" at their Spring Performance), and Caren Geberer, Associate Director, who ran a Writers Workshop that I attended.

Other encouraging friends and readers: Evie Talbot, whose comments were so enthusiastic that I was sorry I couldn't use them as a publisher's blurb; Rabbi Angela Buchdahl of Central Synagogue, Susan Chambers, Barbara Hulsart, Jacqueline Morrison, Sarah Bond, Rebecca Mercer White, Claudia Catania, Marsha Palanci, Marianne Fabre-Lanvin, David Aronson, et al.

And a new definition of gratitude to my team at Memorial Sloan Kettering, who also took the time to read some of my "Sick Humor" essays. Whenever I see Dr. Jedd Wolchok, he always says, "Oh, look who's here — it's the Prednisone Princess!" I also appreciate the ongoing enthusiastic response of Aly Weinstein, and my oncological ophthalmologist; Dr. Francis, who always responded immediately with excited comments; and Dr. Jennifer Hay, who exhorted me to write for a wider audience.

And finally, I have to include a quote from an email I recently received from another member of Dr. Wolchok's team, Kerry Williams. When they were doing rounds in the hospital this month and stopped in my room, Dr. Wolchok introduced me to Kerry and instructed me to send "Prednisone Princess Diaries" to her. Which I did, as soon as I got home for the hospital.

"I absolutely *love* the piece on Prednisone," she wrote back. "I will have to share with our team, it is so perfectly written and depicts all the side effects of the drug. It also gave me clear insight on what we 'do' to patients with medications we give."

Her response makes it all worth it.

Aileen Robbins, January 2019

Afterword

My mother, Aileen Robbins died on March 23, 2018. She was at home in New York surrounded by family on a beautiful Saturday morning. During her final week, she remained actively involved with the details of her book, meeting with her editor, suggesting copy changes, and reviewing the cover design. On Friday evening, we read her stories from her book, ending with one of her (and my) favorites, *Nice Bacon and Eggs*.

Ariel K. Fantasia

www.ingramcontent.com/pod-product-compliance
Lightning Source LLC
Chambersburg PA
CBHW030635150426
42811CB00077B/2108/J
9781732391550